Actual Minds, Possible Worlds

Jerome Bruner

Harvard University Press
Cambridge, Massachusetts
and London, England

Printed in the United States of America

Library of Congress Cataloging-in-Publication Data

Bruner, Jerome Seymour.
Actual minds, possible worlds.

Bibliography: p.
Includes index.
1. Psychology—Philosophy—Addresses, essays, lectures. 2. Psychology and literature—Addresses, essays, lectures. 3. Psycholinguistics—Addresses, essays, lectures. I. Title.
BF38.B75 1986 150 85-27297
ISBN 0-674-00365-9 (alk. paper) (cloth)
ISBN 0-674-00366-7 (paper)

To my grandson, Mark Linehan Bruner

Contents

Preface

This book grew out of an effort to edit a collection of essays written between 1980 and 1984. Each of the essays had been prepared for a particular occasion and a particular audience. The essays would simply be edited better to express what they had intended to say. But I discovered upon rereading them that each was an occasion-bound expression of a general point of view that I had been struggling to formulate during those years.

I decided instead to write them all over again, this time keeping my eye more on the general point of view they were trying to express, and less on the demands of the particular occasions. But all of the chapters save two started their lives as responses to particular invitations, and I should like to record my gratitude to my hosts.

"Approaching the Literary" is new, written to make clearer to myself the nature of the enterprise. "Two Modes of Thought" began as an invited address to the American Psychological Association. "Possible Castles" was first given as the Gordon Mills Lecture at the University of Texas in Austin. "The Transactional Self" had a double origin: in the Bender Lecture given in New York, and in another presented to the Erikson Institute in Chicago. "The Inspiration of Vygotsky" had its start as a presentation to a symposium on Vygotsky at the Center for Psycho-social Studies in Chicago. "Psychological Reality," like the opening essay, was written for the present book to clear up matters outstanding in my own mind, though it carries some echoes of the Katz-Newcomb Lecture given at the University of Michigan. "Nelson

Goodman's Worlds" (with Carol Feldman as co-author) was written for the *New York Review of Books* and is the exception in this volume: it is virtually unchanged from its original form. "Thought and Emotion," in contrast, started as a keynote address to the Jean Piaget Society, though nothing remains of the original. "The Language of Education" first saw life as the Bode Lecture at Ohio State University. And, finally, "Developmental Theory as Culture" grew from a seed in the form of another invited address to the American Psychological Association. I am deeply grateful to my hosts on those occasions and to the colleagues and students who gave so freely of their comments. I hope they will find echoes of them in this book.

I owe a special debt to two foundations that supported my work during the period when this book was growing. The first is to the Sloan Foundation, which provided me with an initial grant to explore the nature of narrative as a mode of thought and as an art form. The Spencer Foundation generously provided a later grant for the pursuit of these studies, the first results of which are presented in several of the chapters of this book.

Two other institutions have my gratitude. One of them, the Graduate Faculty of the New School for Social Research, is my academic home. It has provided me with colleagues, students, and the goad of classes to teach. The other, the New York Institute for the Humanities at New York University, fills the bill of club, pub, and forum. Its lunches, seminars, and lectures have provided me with companionship as complex as it has been rich.

I particularly want to thank students and colleagues who participated in seminars on narrative theory and practice at the New School and at the Institute, as well as visitors who came from afar to present their ideas to us. I am especially indebted as well to the members of my research group, some of whose work is presented in Chapter 2: Alison Armstrong, Sara Davis, Gwyneth Lewis, Pamela Moorhead, David Polonoff, James Walkup, Susan Weisser, and Walter Zahorodny.

There are many intellectual debts to friends—more of them than I can ever mention, much less pay back. Eric Wanner, Richard Sennett, Dan Stern, David Rieff, Arien Mack, Oliver Sacks, John Guare, Stanley Diamond, Bonnie Borenstein, Henri Zukier, Janet Malcolm, and Diana Trilling are among those to whom I owe most. So too my squash partner, William Taylor, who can talk convincing historiography between games even when he is behind. I also want to thank my editor, Camille Smith, for her unfailing good humor and good advice, and my publisher and friend Arthur Rosenthal, who proposed the book in the first place. Some of the themes that inform Part One of the book were given a first tryout at the University of Konstanz in June 1985, and I want particularly to thank Tom Luckmann and Wolfgang Iser for their helpful comments. Pamela Moorhead helped ready the manuscript for the Press with skill and patience.

To Carol Feldman I owe a particular debt. She has been supporter, critic, and a prodigious source of ideas and inspiration.

To say that all human thinking is essentially of two kinds—reasoning on the one hand, and narrative, descriptive, contemplative thinking on the other—is to say only what every reader's experience will corroborate.

William James

Part One

Two Natural Kinds

1

Approaching the Literary

Czeslaw Milosz begins his Charles Eliot Norton Lectures, delivered at Harvard in 1981–82, with a comment that is both emblem and warning:

> Many learned books on poetry have been written, and they find, at least in the countries of the West, more readers than does poetry itself. This is not a good sign, even if it may be explained both by the brilliance of their authors and by their zeal in assimilating scientific disciplines which today enjoy universal respect. A poet who would like to compete with those mountains of erudition would have to pretend he possesses more self-knowledge than poets are allowed to have.

For the three essays in Part One of this book are about poetry in one or another of its guises. And together they constitute yet another of those efforts to look at art through the glass of those respected "scientific disciplines."

Milosz goes on: "Frankly, all my life I have been in the power of a daimonion, and how the poems dictated by him came into being I do not quite understand. That is the reason why, in my years of teaching Slavic literatures, I have limited myself to the history of literature, trying to avoid poetics." I doubt we can read the demon's voice either, or even reconstruct it from the text. Freud, admitting the same point in "The Poet and the Daydream," urges, nonetheless, that the poem in its own right can tell us much about the nature of mind, even if it fails to yield up the secret of its creation. Dostoevski's mystical genius, Joyce's treacherous ways with language, these can still be studied with profit, though we do not know their inspiration. No literary sciences (any more than any natural sciences) can penetrate particular moments of inspired creation. But however they came into existence, the worlds of *The Secret Sharer* or of Stephen Daedalus in *A Portrait of the Artist as a Young Man* constitute texts as well as worlds. And these texts are worthy of the disciplined attention of anybody who seeks to understand the symbolic worlds that the writer creates. If we bring to bear upon these texts the most powerful instruments of literary, linguistic, and psychological analysis, we may yet understand not only what makes a story, but what makes it great. Who would deny that Aristotle's *Poetics* helped us understand tragedy, or that two millennia later, others illuminated different literary landscapes—Roman Jakobson the sound structure of poetry, Vladimir Propp the morphology of folktales, Kenneth Burke the dramatistic "grammar of motives," and even Roland Barthes (for all his self-mockery) the "writerly" text. This is the domain of literary theory.

But there is a second step in literary analysis that is rarely taken. Once we have characterized a text in terms of its structure, its historical context, its linguistic form, its genre, its multiple levels of meaning, and the rest, we may still wish to discover how and in what ways the text affects the reader and, indeed, what produces such effects on the reader as do occur. What makes great stories reverberate with such liveliness in our ordinarily mundane minds? What gives great fiction its power: what in the text and what in the reader? Can a "psychology" of literature describe systematically what happens when a reader enters the Dublin of Stephen Daedalus through the text of *Portrait*?

The usual way of approaching such issues is to invoke psychological processes or mechanisms that operate in "real life." Characters in story are said to be compelling by virtue of our capacity for "identification" or because, in their ensemble, they represent the cast of characters that we, the readers, carry unconsciously within us. Or, on the linguistic side, literature is said to affect us by virtue of its tropes—for example, by metaphor and synecdoche that evoke zestful imaginative play. But such proposals explain so much that they explain very little. They fail to tell why some stories succeed and some fail to engage the reader. And above all, they fail to provide an account of the processes of reading and of entering a story. There have been efforts to explore these processes more directly, as in I. A. Richards's *Practical Criticism* where actual alternative "readings" of poems were examined, but such efforts have been rare and, on the whole, psychologically not well informed. Perhaps the task is too daunting.

Let me illustrate some of the challenges—and suggest why I think that, for all its dauntingness, the task is both possible and worthwhile, and why it might shed light not only on literary issues but on psychological ones beyond the limits of the psychology of literature. Take first the issue of alternative (or multiple) readings of a story or, for that matter, of any text. It is an ancient issue and has its origin in both classical linguistics and the interpreting of biblical texts. Nicholas of Lyra proposed many centuries ago, for example, that biblical texts are amenable to four levels of interpretation: *litera, moralis, allegoria,* and *anagogia,* the literal, the ethical, the historical, and the mystical. Literary and general linguists have always insisted that no text, no story can be understood at a single level. Roman Jakobson, for example, urged that all meaning is a form of translation, and that multiple translation (polysemy) is the rule rather than the exception: an utterance can be conceived of as referential, as expressive, as conative (in the sense of a speech act), as poetic, as phatic (contact preserving), and as metalinguistic. And Roland Barthes in *S/Z* (the analysis of a single text, Balzac's *Sarrasine*) illustrates how a novel achieves its meaning in the interplay of the interpretations yielded by at least five different "codes." What Nicholas of Lyra, Jakobson, and Barthes are saying, in effect, is that one *can* read and interpret texts in various ways, indeed in various ways simultaneously. Indeed, the prevailing view is that we *must* read and interpret in some multiple way if any "literary" meaning is to be extracted from a text. But in fact we know little about how readers actually do so—we know precious little indeed about the "reader-in-the-text" as a psychological process.

For the psychologist of literature, the theoretical analysis of "text interpretation" (by whomever formulated, and whatever the textual data base of the analysis) yields only hypotheses about actual readers. Do all readers assign multiple meanings to stories? And how can we characterize these multiple meanings? What kinds of category systems best capture this "meaning attribution" process, and how idiosyncratic is it? Is interpretation affected by genre, and what does genre mean psychologically (a matter to which I shall turn presently)? And *how* are multiple meanings triggered? What is there in the text that produces this multiple effect, and how can one characterize the susceptibility of readers to polysemy? These are the kinds of questions we must ask as *psychologists* of literature, and I shall return to them in the next chapter.

Take the question of genre, another ancient issue in literary theory and one that still preoccupies literary scholars in a major way. Aristotle put his hand to the question in the *Poetics*, and his characterization of comedy and of tragedy in terms of both character and plot form is still a living part of literary theory. And Freud or no Freud, Aristotle's is still an astute psychological (as well as literary) speculation—to which I shall return to often in later chapters. There are many other literary approaches to genre that are psychologically suggestive. For contrast, take the formal distinction between epic and lyric offered by Austin Warren and René Wellek in their classic *Theory of Literature*: epic is the poetry of past tense, third person; lyric of first person present tense. While it was a distinction offered only as text characterization, it is interesting in more than a purely linguistic sense. Is it the case, for example, that the generic "unity" in the world of a fictional text depends upon the maintenance of a space-time structure, and that this unity requires consistent marking of tense and person? Is "psychological" genre constituted of such space-time marking: tales-of-others in the past, tales-of-self in the present, and so on? We do not know the answers to such questions, but in the following chapters I shall explore ways of pursuing them.

One gets a sense of the psychology of genre by listening to readers "tell back" a story they have just read or spontaneously "tell" a story about a "happening" in their own lives. "Telling back" a Conrad story, one reader will turn it into a yarn of adventure, another into a moral tale about duplicity, and a third into a case study of a *Doppelganger*. The text from which they started was the same. Genre seems to be a way of both organizing the structure of events and organizing the telling of them—a way that can be used for one's own storytelling or, indeed, for "placing" stories one is reading or hearing. Something in the actual text "triggers" an interpretation of genre in the reader, an interpretation that then dominates the reader's own creation of what Wolfgang Iser calls a "virtual text."

What then are the "triggers" and what are the subjective forms of genre that come to dominate the reader's mind? Is subjective genre merely a convention, and are the triggers little more than literary or semiotic road signs telling the reader what genre it is and what stance to take toward the story? Yet, there is something altogether too universal about tragedy, comedy, epic, tales of deceit, for the explanation of genre to be only a matter of convention. Nor is it fixed and "hard-wired." Anthony Burgess says of "Clay" in Joyce's *Dubliners* that it is a *comic* story. It *can* be read that way. Maria (its principal character) then is seen as a comic bungler caught in the ennui of Dublin. Her illusions about herself then become the stuff of Joycean black comedy. Yes, one can read it as Burgess does, or at least try to.

But stories, in Paul Ricoeur's phrase, are "models for the redescription of the world." But the story is not by itself the model. It is, so to speak, an instantiation of models we carry in our own minds. An undergraduate in a seminar in which I once participated interpreted *Hamlet* as an account of the bungling of a Danish prince who had become "sword happy" at his German university and who was so inept at killing the man he hated that he did in his wisest friend, Polonius, in the process. Yes, this student admitted, the play was a "tragedy," but it was also a bungle (he was in engineering—with passion).

One rereads a story in endlessly changing ways—litera, moralis, allegoria, anagogia. (The young engineer was at moralis.) The alternate ways of reading may battle one another, marry one another, mock one another in the reader's mind. There is something in the telling, something in the plot that triggers this "genre conflict" in readers (see Chapter 2). The story goes nowhere and everywhere. So Frank Kermode, in distinguishing *sjuzet* and *fabula* (the linear incidents that make the plot, versus the timeless, motionless, underlying theme) remarks that the power of great stories is in the dialectical interaction they establish between the two: "the fusion of scandal and miracle." So while the reader begins by placing a story in one genre (and that may have powerful effects on his reading), he changes as he goes. The actual text is unchanged; the virtual text (to paraphrase Iser) changes almost moment to moment in the act of reading.

If we then ask about the nature and role of *psychological* genre—the reader's conception of what kind of story or text he is encountering or "recreating"—we are in fact asking not only a morphological question about the actual text, but also a question about the interpretive processes that are loosed by the text in the reader's mind.

❧

Twenty-odd years ago, engaged in research on the psychological nature and development of thought, I had one of those mild crises so endemic to students of mind. The Apollonian and the Dionysian, the logical and the intuitive, were at war. Gustave Theodor Fechner, the founder of modern experimental psychology, had called them the *Tagesansicht* and *Nachtansicht*. My own research had taken me more and more deeply into the study of logical inference, the strategies by which ordinary people penetrate to the logical structure of the regularities they encounter in a world that they create through the very exercise of mind that they use for exploring it.

I also read novels, went to films, let myself fall under the spell of Camus, Conrad, Robbe-Grillet, Sartre, Burgess, Bergman, Joyce, Antonioni. From time to time, almost as if to keep some balance between night and day, I wrote essays—about Freud, the modern novel, metaphor, mythology, painting. They were informal and "literary" rather than "systematic" in form, however psychologically motivated they may have been.

Eventually, I published these "fugitive" essays as a book: *On Knowing: Essays for the Left Hand*. It was a relief to get the book out, though I do not think its publication changed my way of working much. By day, the *Tagesansicht* prevailed: my psychological research continued. At night there were novels and poems and plays. The crisis had passed.

Meanwhile, psychology itself had gone through changes, and, doubtless for the good, the voices of the left hand and of the right came more publicly and raucously into discussion with each other. The cognitive revolution in psychology, for one thing, had made it possible to consider the question of how knowledge and experience in their myriad forms were organized. And since language is our most powerful tool for organizing experience, and indeed, for constituting "realities," the products of language in all their rich variety were coming in for closer scrutiny. By the mid-1970s the social sciences had moved away from their traditional positivist stance toward a more interpretive posture: meaning became the central focus—how the word was interpreted, by what codes meaning was regulated, in what sense culture itself could be treated as a "text" that participants "read" for their own guidance.

And by the mid-1970s, with the Chomskian fervor spent, linguistics returned with more powerful tools to its classical concern with the *uses* of language—among them its use to create the illusions of reality that make fiction. There followed a torrent of research, some obscure and some enlightening, addressing the great themes of "poetics" in the spirit of Jakobson and the Prague School. In time French structuralism—with Claude Lévi-Strauss taking the lead with his analyses of myth—came to dominate literary theory, only to be toppled by the more functionalist approach of the later Barthes, of Derrida, of Greimas, and of the deconstructionist critics (see Chapter 2).

These developments (and more of them to be recounted later) opened new psychological perspectives. For perhaps it is true, as academic psychologists like to say about themselves, that psychology has the courage of other peoples' convictions. Psychoanalysts, following the earlier lead of George Klein, began inquiring whether the object of analysis was not so much archaeologically to reconstruct a life as it was to help the patient construct a more contradiction-free and generative narrative of it. In which case, what constituted a narrative, or better, a *good* narrative? And academic psychologists, inspired by the lead of David Rumelhart, began to work on "story grammars," formal descriptions of the minimum structure that yielded stories or storylike sequences. And as if part of a *Zeitgeist,* even historians and historiographers, not notable for innovative courage, were again brooding about the powers of narrative history—Francis Parkman, say, in contrast to an analytic social economist sorting over the same period.

My old interest was rekindled. Setting out to sample this mass of new work, I discovered that there were two styles of approaching narrative, a discovery pressed upon me while I was teaching concurrently two seminars on narrative. One of them, at the New School for Social Research, was dominated by psychologists. The other, at the New York Institute for the Humanities, was made up of playwrights, poets, novelists, critics, editors. Both seminars were interested in psychological questions; both were interested in literary questions. Both were interested in readers and in writers. Both were interested in texts. But one group, the psychologists, was dedicated to working "top-down," the other to working "bottom-up." It is a distinction worth exploring, one that foretells something about the conflict one senses in working on narrative and on the psychology of literature generally.

Top-down partisans take off from a theory about story, about mind, about writers, about readers. The theory may be anchored wherever: in psychoanalysis, in structural linguistics, in a theory of memory, in the philosophy of history. Armed with an hypothesis, the top-down partisan swoops on this text and that, searching for instances (and less often counter-instances) of what he hopes will be a right "explanation." In skilled and dispassionate hands, it is a powerful way to work. It is the way of the linguist, the social scientist, and of science generally, but it instills habits of work that always risk producing results that are insensitive to the contexts in which they were dug up. It partakes of one of the modes of thought to which I shall turn in the next chapter—the paradigmatic.

Bottom-up partisans march to a very different tune. Their approach is focused on a particular piece of work: a story, a novel, a poem, even a line. They take it as their morsel of reality and explore it to reconstruct or deconstruct it. They are in search of the implicit theory in Conrad's construction of *Heart of Darkness* or in the worlds that Flaubert constructs. It is not that they are occupied biographically with Conrad or with Flaubert, although they do not turn a tin ear to such matters, nor are they so taken with the new criticism that they look only at the text and its artifices, though they are concerned with that too. Rather, the effort is to *read* a text for its meanings, and by doing so to elucidate the art of its author. They do not forswear the guidance of psychoanalytic theory or of Jakobsonian poetics or even of the philosophy of language in pursuing their quest. But their quest is not to prove or disprove a theory, but to explore the world of a particular literary work.

Partisans of the top-down approach bewail the particularity of those who proceed bottom-up. The latter deplore the abstract nonwriterliness of the former. The two do not, alas, talk much to each other.

In the two essays that follow, I shall satisfy neither side, and, even worse, I can see no reason to apologize for it. Nor can I justify it by arguing that when we know enough, the two approaches will fuse. I do not think so. The most that I can claim is that, as with the stereoscope, depth is better achieved by looking from two points at once.

2

Two Modes of Thought

Let me begin by setting out my argument as baldly as possible, better to examine its basis and its consequences. It is this. There are two modes of cognitive functioning, two modes of thought, each providing distinctive ways of ordering experience, of constructing reality. The two (though complementary) are irreducible to one another. Efforts to reduce one mode to the other or to ignore one at the expense of the other inevitably fail to capture the rich diversity of thought.

Each of the ways of knowing, moreover, has operating principles of its own and its own criteria of well-formedness. They differ radically in their procedures for verification. A good story and a well-formed argument are different natural kinds. Both can be used as means for convincing another. Yet what they convince *of* is fundamentally different: arguments convince one of their truth, stories of their lifelikeness. The one verifies by eventual appeal to procedures for establishing formal and empirical proof. The other establishes not truth but verisimilitude. It has been claimed that the one is a refinement of or an abstraction from the other. But this must be either false or true only in the most unenlightening way.

They function differently, as already noted, and the structure of a well-formed logical argument differs radically from that of a well-wrought story. Each, perhaps, is a specialization or transformation of simple exposition, by which statements of fact are converted into statements implying causality. But the types of causality implied in the two modes are palpably different. The term *then* functions differently in the logical proposition "if x, then y" and in the narrative *recit* "The king died, and then the queen died." One leads to a search for universal truth conditions, the other for likely particular connections between two events—mortal grief, suicide, foul play. While it is true that the world of a story (to achieve verisimilitude) must conform to canons of logical consistency, it can use violations of such consistency as a basis of drama—as in the novels of Kafka, where nonlogical arbitrariness in the social order provides the engine of drama, or in the plays of Pirandello or Beckett, where the identity operator, a = a, is cunningly violated to create multiple perspectives. And by the same token, the arts of rhetoric include the use of dramatic instantiation as a means of clinching an argument whose basis is principally logical.

But for all that, a story (allegedly true or allegedly fictional) is judged for its goodness as a story by criteria that are of a different kind from those used to judge a logical argument as adequate or correct. We all know by now that many scientific and mathematical hypotheses start their lives as little stories or metaphors, but they reach their scientific maturity by a process of conversion into verifiability, formal or empirical, and their power at maturity does not rest upon their dramatic origins. Hypothesis creation (in contrast to hypothesis testing) remains a tantalizing mystery—so much so that sober philosophers of science, like Karl Popper, characterize science as consisting principally of the falsification of hypotheses, no matter the source whence the hypothesis has come. Perhaps Richard Rorty is right in characterizing the mainstream of Anglo-American philosophy (which, on the whole, he rejects) as preoccupied with the epistemological question of how to know truth—which he contrasts with the broader question of how we come to endow experience with meaning, which is the question that preoccupies the poet and the storyteller.

Let me quickly and lightly characterize the two modes so that I may get on more precisely with the matter. One mode, the paradigmatic or logico-scientific one, attempts to fulfill the ideal of a formal, mathematical system of description and explanation. It employs categorization or conceptualization and the operations by which categories are established, instantiated, idealized, and related one to the other to form a system. Its armamentarium of connectives includes on the formal side such ideas as conjunction and disjunction, hyperonymy and hyponymy, strict implication, and the devices by which general propositions are extracted from statements in their particular contexts. At a gross level, the logico-scientific mode (I shall call it paradigmatic hereafter) deals in general causes, and in their establishment, and makes use of procedures to assure verifiable reference and to test for empirical truth. Its language is regulated by requirements of consistency and noncontradiction. Its domain is defined not only by observables to which its basic statements relate, but also by the set of possible worlds that can be logically generated and tested against observables—that is, it is driven by principled hypotheses.

We know a very great deal about the paradigmatic mode of thinking, and there have been developed over the millennia powerful prosthetic devices for helping us carry on with its work: logic, mathematics, sciences, and automata for operating in these fields as painlessly and swiftly as possible. We also know a fair amount about how children who are weak initially at the paradigmatic mode grow up to be fairly good at it when they can be induced to use it. The imaginative application of the paradigmatic mode leads to good theory, tight analysis, logical proof, sound argument, and empirical discovery guided by reasoned hypothesis. But paradigmatic "imagination" (or intuition) is not the same as the imagination of the novelist or poet. Rather, it is the ability to see possible formal connections before one is able to prove them in any formal way.

The imaginative application of the narrative mode leads instead to good stories, gripping drama, believable (though not necessarily "true") historical accounts. It deals in human or human-like intention and action and the vicissitudes and consequences that mark their course. It strives to put its timeless miracles into the particulars of experience, and to locate the experience in time and place. Joyce thought of the particularities of the story as epiphanies of the ordinary. The paradigmatic mode, by contrast, seeks to transcend the particular by higher and higher reaching for abstraction, and in the end disclaims in principle any explanatory value at all where the particular is concerned. There is a heartlessness to logic: one goes where one's premises and conclusions and observations take one, give or take some of the blindnesses that even logicians are prone to. Scientists, perhaps because they rely on familiar stories to fill in the gaps of their knowledge, have a harder time in practice. But their salvation is to wash the stories away when causes can be substituted for them. Paul Ricoeur argues that narrative is built upon concern for the human condition: stories reach sad or comic or absurd denouements, while theoretical arguments are simply conclusive or inconclusive. In contrast to our vast knowledge of how science and logical reasoning proceed, we know precious little in any formal sense about how to make good stories.

Perhaps one of the reasons for this is that story must construct two landscapes simultaneously. One is the landscape of action, where the constituents are the arguments of action: agent, intention or goal, situation, instrument, something corresponding to a "story grammar." The other landscape is the landscape of consciousness: what those involved in the action know, think, or feel, or do not know, think, or feel. The two landscapes are essential and distinct: it is the difference between Oedipus sharing Jocasta's bed before and after he learns from the messenger that she is his mother.

In this sense, psychic reality dominates narrative and any reality that exists beyond the awareness of those involved in the story is put there by the author with the object of creating dramatic effect. Indeed, it is an invention of modern novelists and playwrights to create a world made up entirely of the psychic realities of the protagonists, leaving knowledge of the "real" world in the realm of the implicit. So writers as different as Joyce and Melville share the characteristic of not "disclosing" aboriginal realities but leaving them at the horizon of the story as matters of supposition—or, as we shall see, of *pre*supposition.

Science—particularly theoretical physics—also proceeds by constructing worlds in a comparable way, by "inventing" the facts (or world) against which the theory must be tested. But the striking difference is that, from time to time, there are moments of testing when, for example, light can be shown to be bent or neutrinos must be shown to leave marks in a cloud chamber. It may indeed be the case, as Quine has urged, that physics is 99 percent speculation and 1 percent observation. But the world making involved in its speculations is of a different order from what story making does. Physics must eventuate in predicting something that is testably right, however much it may speculate. Stories have no such need for testability. Believability in a story is of a different order than the believability of even the speculative parts of physical theory. If we apply Popper's criterion of falsifiability to a story as a test of its goodness, we are guilty of misplaced verification.

❧

Having said that much about how the two modes can be distinguished one from the other, let me now focus almost entirely on the less understood of the pair: on narrative. And as I remarked in the preceding chapter, I shall want to concentrate on narrative, so to speak, at its far reach: as an art form. William James comments in his Gifford Lectures, *The Varieties of Religious Experience*, that to study religion one should study the most religious man at his most religious moment. I shall try to follow his advice with respect to narrative but, perhaps, with a Platonic twist. The great works of fiction that transform narrative into an art form come closest to revealing "purely" the deep structure of the narrative mode in expression. The same claim can be made for science and mathematics: they reveal most plainly (and purely) the deep structure of paradigmatic thought. And perhaps James intended his dictum in the same sense, in spite of his anti-Platonism.

There is another reason, aside from the Platonic, for pursuing this course. If one takes the view (as I shall in Chapter 5) that human mental activity depends for its full expression upon being linked to a cultural tool kit—a set of prosthetic devices, so to speak—then we are well advised when studying mental activity to take into account the tools employed in that activity. As primatologists tell us, this amplification by cultural tools is the hallmark of human skills, and we overlook it in our research with peril. And so, if one wishes to study the psychology of mathematics (as, say, G. Polya did), one studies the works of trained and gifted mathematicians, with particular emphasis on the heuristics and the formalisms they use to give form to their mathematical intuitions.

By the same token, one does well to study the work of trained and gifted writers if one is to understand what it is that makes good stories powerful or compelling. Anybody (at almost any age) can tell a story—and it is altogether good that story grammarians, so called, are studying the minimal structure needed to create a story. And anybody (again, at almost any age) can "do" some mathematics. But great fiction, like great mathematics, requires the transformation of intuitions into expressions in a symbolic system—natural language or some artificialized form of it. The forms of expression that emerge, the discourse that carries the story, or the calculus that depicts a mathematical relation—these are crucial for understanding the differences between an inchoate account of a bad marriage and *Madame Bovary*, between a clumsily argued justification and an elegant and powerful derivation of a logical proof. I think I have said all that needs saying on this point, a point addressed more to psychologists than to literary theorists. The former, perhaps, will quarrel with the point out of deference to the reductionism of science. The latter will almost certainly find the point almost bizarrely obvious.

❧

Narrative deals with the vicissitudes of human intentions. And since there are myriad intentions and endless ways for them to run into trouble—or so it would seem—there should be endless kinds of stories. But, surprisingly, this seems not to be the case. One view has it that lifelike narratives start with a canonical or "legitimate" steady state, which is breached, resulting in a crisis, which is terminated by a redress, with recurrence of the cycle an open possibility. Literary theorists as various as Victor Turner (an anthropologist), Tzvetan Todorov, Hayden White (an historian), and Vladimir Propp (a folklorist) suggest that there is some such constraining deep structure to narrative, and that good stories are well-formed particular realizations of it. Not all literary scholars take this view—Barbara Herrnstein-Smith being a notable dissenting voice.

If it were the case that there are limits on the kinds of stories, it could mean either that the limits are inherent in the minds of writers and/or readers (what one is able to tell or to understand), or that the limits are a matter of convention. If it were the former, if the limits on story were innate, then it would be difficult to explain the eruptions of innovation that illuminate the course of literary history. And if it were the latter, the heavy hand of convention, that limited the nature of story, then it would be just as difficult to explain why there is so much recognizable similarity in tales from all lands, and so much historical continuity within any particular language whose literatures have gone through changes as dramatic as, say, the French or English or Russian.

The arguments pro and con are, somehow, more interesting than conclusive. Their conclusiveness is flawed not only by literary innovation but, I suspect, by the impossibility of deciding whether, say,

Joyce's *Ulysses* or Beckett's *Molloy* trilogy fits a particular formula or not. Aside from all that, what level of interpretation of a story shall we take to represent its "deep structure"—litera, moralis, allegoria, or anagogia? And whose interpretation: Jung's, Foucault's, Northrop Frye's? And when, as with antinovel novels, a writer (like Calvino, say) exploits his reader's story expectations by flouting them artfully, does that count as violating or conforming to the canonical form?

And as if this were not enough, there is the question of the discourse into which the story is woven and the two aspects of story (to which we have already alluded): the *fabula* and the *sjuzet,* the timeless and the sequenced. Which is constrained, and in what ways? That there may be a structure to time-worn folktales or to myths, a matter to which I shall revert later, nobody will deny. But do these narratives provide a universal structure for all fictions? For Alain Robbe-Grillet or, to take an instance where it is even difficult to decide whether the book is a novel or an exercise in criticism, for Julian Barnes's *Flaubert's Parrot*?

I think we would do well with as loose fitting a constraint as we can manage concerning what a story must "be" to be a story. And the one that strikes me as most serviceable is the one with which we began: narrative deals with the vicissitudes of intention.

I propose this not only because it leaves the theorist with a certain flexibility but because it has a "primitiveness" that is appealing. By primitive I mean simply that one can make a strong argument for the irreducible nature of the concept of intention (much as Kant did for the concept of causation). That is to say, intention is immediately and intuitively recognizable: it seems to require for its recognition no complex or sophisticated interpretive act on the part of the beholder. The evidence for such a claim is compelling.

There is a celebrated monograph, little known outside academic psychology, written a generation ago by the Belgian student of perception, Baron Michotte. By cinematic means, he demonstrated that when objects move with respect to one another within highly limited constraints, we *see* causality. An object moves toward another, makes contact with it, and the second object is seen to move in a compatible direction: we see one object "launching" another. Time-space relations can variously be arranged so that one object can be seen as "dragging" another, or "deflecting" it, and so on. These are "primitive" perceptions, and they are quite irresistible: we *see* cause.

To answer Hume's objection that such causal experiences derive from association, Alan Leslie repeated the Michotte demonstrations with six-month-old babies. His procedure measured signs of surprise in the infant, which expresses itself in a variety of registerable ways from facial expression to changes in heart rate and blood pressure. Leslie showed the infants a sequence of cinematic presentations that in their space-time arrangement were seen by adults as caused. He would then intersperse one noncausal presentation that was outside the prescribed Michotte space-time limits—and the baby would show startled surprise. The same effect could be achieved by following a noncausal sequence of presentations with a causal one. In each case, Leslie argued, there was some qualitative change in the experience of the infant that led to "dishabituation" and surprise. Note that a change in space-time arrangement of the displays that was as large as the one used to shift category produced no effect if it was within the category of causality. Michotte's work and Leslie's follow-up provide powerful arguments for the irreducibility of causality as a "mental category" in the Kantian sense.

Can intentionality as a concept be shown to be as primitive? Fritz Heider and Marianne Simmel have also used a "bare" animated film to demonstrate the irresistibility of "perceived intention" in the form of a scenario involving a small moving triangle, a small moving circle, a large moving square, and a box-like empty rectangle—whose movements are irresistibly seen as two lovers being pursued by a large bully who, upon being thwarted, breaks up the house in which he has tried to find them. Judith Ann Stewart, more recently, has shown that it is possible to arrange the space-time relationship of simple figures to produce apparent intention or "animacy." We plainly *see* "search," "goal seeking," "persistence in overcoming obstacles"—see them as intention-driven. Interestingly, from the point of view of Propp's pioneering work on the structure of folktales (to which we shall come presently), the perception of animacy is induced by varying direction and speed of motion of an object with respect to an obstacle.

Unfortunately, we do not yet have the analogue experiment on apparent intention for Leslie's baby experiments on apparent causality. It will come soon enough. If it should yield positive results, then we would have to conclude that "intention and its vicissitudes" constitute a primitive category system in terms of which experience is organized, at least as primitive as the category system of causality. I say "at least," for the fact remains that the evidence of children's animism suggests that their more primitive category is intention—physically caused events being seen as psychically intended, as in the early experiments that earned Piaget his first worldwide acclaim.

❧

But such experiments, while they tell us about the primitiveness of the idea of intention, tell us nothing about the discourse that converts an unworded narrative into powerful and haunting stories. What is it in the telling or writing of a tale that produces Jakobson's *literaturnost*? In the *telling* there must be "triggers" that release responses in the reader's mind, that transform a banal fabula into a masterpiece of literary narrative. Obviously, the language of the discourse is critical, but even before that there is plot, plot and its structure. Whatever the medium—whether words, cinema, abstract animation, theater—one can always distinguish between the fabula or basic story stuff, the events to be related in the narrative, and the "plot" or sjuzet, the story as told by linking the events together. The plot is how and in what order the reader becomes aware of what happened. And the "same" story can be told in different sequence. This means, of course, that there must be transformations of some kind that permit a common base structure of story to be handled in different meaning-preserving sequences.

What can we say about the deep structure of stories—the story stuff, or fabula, that lends itself to different orders of presentation? Could it be the kind of structure that I examined a moment ago and earlier attributed to Victor Turner, Hayden White, Vladimir Propp, and Tzvetan Todorov? That is to say, one "primitive" fabula involves the breach of a legitimate state of affairs, the break then creating a crisis that is nipped in the bud or that persists until there is redress? If there were a corresponding structure in the minds of readers, cinema viewers, and playgoers, then such a fabula could be plotted in linear order, in flashbacks, or even *in medias res,* starting virtually anywhere (as Robbe-Grillet succeeds in doing for film and novel, and as, say, Michel Leiris does in his "experimental" antinarrative autobiography)? We do not have to take a stand on how many such fabula there are (as many, for example, as Jung's archetypes?), only that they have some sort of being in the beholder's mind that permits him to recognize them in whatever expression encountered.

But there is something more to it than that. Kenneth Burke argues that "story stuff" involves *characters* in *action* with intentions or *goals* in *settings* using particular *means*. Drama is generated, he claims, when there is an imbalance in the "ratio" of these constituents. That is to say, a character (say Nora in *A Doll's House*) is in an inappropriate setting, or an action does not warrant the goal to which it is leading a character.

Yet, neither breach, crisis, and redress, nor imbalances in a Burkeian pentad, are sufficient descriptions of "story stuff." For there are elements of story that rest not upon action and interaction but upon character as such. Conrad's novels provide a good example. Jim's inscrutability (even to the narrator who "tells" his story) is central to the drama of *Lord Jim*. In *The Secret Sharer*, the young captain's fascinated obsession with Leggatt drives the story. Some readers actually propose that Leggatt is an imaginary *Doppelganger* who exists only in the captain's mind. Perhaps, as with Aristotle's recipe for tragedy in the *Poetics*, drama is a working out of character in action in a plot constrained by a setting.

Yet this too cannot be a full account if we heed Propp's argument that, in the folktale, character is a *function* of a highly constrained plot, the chief role of a character being to play out a plot role as hero, false hero, helper, villain, and so on. For while it may be the case that in the time-smoothed folktale story-stuff determines character (and therefore character cannot be central), it is equally true that in the "modern" novel plot is derived from the working out of character in a particular setting (one of the earliest theorists of modernism, therefore, being Aristotle on tragedy!).

Greimas's view is that a primitive or irreducible feature of story (whatever else it may include) is that it occurs jointly on the plane of action and in the subjectivity of the protagonists. And perhaps this is why deceit, guile, and misunderstanding are to be found so often in myths and folktales from "Little Red Riding Hood" to "Perseus and the Gorgon" and, at the same time, lie at the heart of so many modern novels and plays.

Psychologically, the "dual landscape" view is appealing in suggesting how the reader is helped to enter the life and mind of the protagonists:

their consciousnesses are the magnets for empathy. The matching of "inner" vision and "outer" reality is, moreover, a classic human plight. It grips the child hearing how the Big Bad Wolf tries to deceive and then is unmasked by Red Riding Hood, or the adult reading Joyce's "Araby," suffering the humiliation of the young boy when his dreams of a gift for the neighbor girl fade in the tawdry atmosphere of the fairground closing.

In any case, the fabula of story—its timeless underlying theme—seems to be a unity that incorporates at least three constituents. It contains a *plight* into which *characters* have fallen as a result of intentions that have gone awry either because of circumstances, of the "character of characters," or most likely of the interaction between the two. And it requires an uneven distribution of underlying consciousness among the characters with respect to the plight. What gives the story its unity is the manner in which plight, characters, and consciousness interact to yield a structure that has a start, a development, and a "sense of an ending." Whether it is sufficient to characterize this unified structure as *steady state, breach, crisis, redress* is difficult to know. It is certainly not *necessary* to do so, for what one seeks in story structure is precisely how plight, character, and consciousness are integrated. Better to leave the issue open and to approach the matter with an open mind.

❧

Language, to whatever use it may be put, has the design feature of being organized on different levels, each level providing constituents for the level above which dominates it. As Jakobson noted in his classic analysis of the sound system of speech, the distinctive features of speech sound are determined by the phonemes that they constitute at the next level up; phonemes are combined according to rules at the next level up, the morpheme, and so on.

So too at the levels above sound, for morphemes, lexemes, sentences, speech acts, and discourse. Each level has its form of order, but that order is controlled and modified by the level above it. Since each level is dominated by the level above it, efforts to understand any level on its own have inevitably led to failure. The structure of language is such that it permits us to go from speech sounds through the intermediate levels to the intentions of speech acts and discourse. The path by which we travel that route varies with our objective, and storytelling is a special objective.

In putting any particular expression together, one *selects* words and one *combines* them. *How* one selects and combines will depend on the uses to which one wishes to put an utterance. Jakobson calls these two primitive language-forming acts, selecting and combining, the *vertical* and the *horizontal* axes of language. The vertical axis of selection is dominated by the requirement of preserving or modifying meaning by substituting appropriate words or expressions for one another: *boy, immature male, lad,* and so on. But the rule of substitution goes beyond synonymy to metaphor. What of *colt, lamb, fawn*? Do they fit *boy*? We say it depends on context and objective. And what of larger-order substitutions? Which does better for New York: "the biggest city in North America" or "the harbor at the mouth of the Hudson"? Again, it depends. And what of substituting for *depression: black mood* or "ragged claws scuttling across the floors of silent seas"? There is forever a matter of choice about the vertical axis: whether to preserve reference as literally as possible, whether to create an atmospheric change by metaphor, whether (as Jakobson and the Prague School urged upon poets) to "make it strange" so as to overcome automatic reading.

It is probably the case that scientific or logical writing—or, rather, writing governed by requirements of a scientific argument—tends to choose words with the object of assuring clear and definite reference and literal sense. It is required by the felicity conditions of speech acts of this kind. Litera dominates over moralis and the others. In the telling of a story, one has the selection restriction of representing a referent in the eye of a protagonist-beholder, with a perspective that fits the subjective landscape on which the story is being unfolded, and yet with due regard for the action that is going on. So from the start, the selection of expressions must meet the special requirement of that special form of speech act that is a story—of which more presently, when I consider a crucial idea proposed by Wolfgang Iser.

The second axis, the horizontal axis of combination, is inherent in the generative power of syntax to combine words and phrases. Its most elementary expression is predication or, even more primitively, the juxtaposition of a comment on a topic, when the topic is "given" or taken for granted and the comment is something new added to it. I see a new species of bird and say to my partner: "Some bird. Fantastic." The first element is the topic; the second the comment. Predication is a more evolved form of making comments on topics that permits us to assign a "truth function" to the expression, as in such ordinary sentences as

The boy has a ball.
The boy has a secret.
The boy has a burning ambition.
The boy has a bee in his bonnet.

The boy is the given; the predicate is new. The sentence can now be translated into a formal or logical proposition and tested for its truth value in the context in which the utterance was made.

To the degree that a subject and predicate are "transparent," they can easily be converted into verifiable propositional form; indeed, one common theory of meaning, the verificationist theory, equates meaning with the set of verifiable propositions a predicational statement generates. But there are statements or utterances that combine given and new in a manner that is "strange" or that, in Henry James's sense, contains gaps, or where there is a difficult distance between the two. A good case in point is Eliot's lines

I should have been a pair of ragged claws
Scuttling across the floors of silent seas.

To render these lines literally as "I am depressed with aging" (taking into account the context of the whole of "Prufrock," from which they are extracted) fails to capture the horizontal given-new combination of the poem. Yet, on one interpretation, that may be what they mean—noting that in the vertical axis we have translated "ragged claws . . ." into "depression over aging." To be sure, as Jakobson also insisted, meaning always involves translation. But there is some sense in which neither the literal translation of the new term nor the resulting combination of it with the given term succeeds as a poetic translation. And if we take predicate-like utterances in which both the subject and the predicate are nonliteral, the failure is even more evident, as in these lines from MacNeice:

The sunlight on the garden
Hardens and grows cold.
We cannot cage the minute
Within its nets of gold;
When all is told
We cannot beg for pardon.

It is not only "unclear" how to manage the vertical axis—to what does "sunlight on the garden" refer, and "harden" in this context? "Cage"? And then, "cage the minute," etcetera.

The language of poetry, or perhaps I should say the language of evocation, substitutes metaphors for both given and new, leaving it somewhat ambiguous what they are substitutes for. When the terms are combined, the resulting given-new combination is no longer amenable to being converted into ordinary truth functional propositions. Indeed, at crucial moments it even departs from the "contract" that specifies a clear distinction between given and new in predicative combinations.

So neither vertically nor horizontally does the evocative language of poetry and story conform to the requirements of plain reference or of verifiable predication. Stories of literary merit, to be sure, are about events in a "real" world, but they render that world newly strange, rescue it from obviousness, fill it with gaps that call upon the reader, in Barthes's sense, to become a writer, a composer of a virtual text in response to the actual. In the end, it is the reader who must write for himself what *he* intends to do with the actual text. How, for example, to read these lines from Yeats:

> The brawling of a sparrow in the eaves,
> The brilliant moon and all the milky sky,
> And all that famous harmony of leaves,
> Had blotted out man's image and his cry.

Which brings us directly to Wolfgang Iser's reflections in *The Act of Reading* on what manner of speech act is a narrative. I want to touch on only one part of his argument, one that is central to my own. With respect to narrative, he says, "the reader receives it by composing it." The text itself has structures that are "two-sided": a *verbal* aspect that guides reaction and prevents it from being arbitrary, and an affective aspect that is triggered or "prestructured by the language of the text." But the prestructure is underdetermined: fictional texts are inherently "indeterminate."

> fictional texts constitute their own objects and do not copy something already in existence. For this reason they cannot have the full determinacy of real objects, and indeed, it is the element of indeterminacy that evokes the text to "communicate" with the reader, in the sense that they induce him to participate both in the production and the comprehension of this work's intention.

It is this "relative indeterminacy of a text" that "allows a spectrum of actualizations." And so, "literary texts initiate 'performances' of meaning rather than actually formulating meanings themselves."

And that is what is at the core of literary narrative as a speech act: an utterance or a text whose intention is to initiate and guide a search for meanings among a spectrum of possible meanings. Storytelling, besides, is a speech act whose felicity conditions are unique. The speech act is initiated by giving some indication to a listener or reader, first, that a story is to be recounted; second, that it is true or fictional; and third (optionally), that it fits some genre—a sad story, a moral fable, a comeuppance tale, a particular scandal, a happening in one's life. Beyond that, there is a condition of style: that the form of the discourse in which the story is actualized leaves open the "performance of meaning" in Iser's sense. It is this last condition that brings us directly to the discourse properties of stories, to which I turn now.

Discourse, if Iser is right about narrative speech acts, must depend upon forms of discourse that recruit the reader's imagination—that enlist him in the "performance of meaning under the guidance of the text." Discourse must make it possible for the reader to "write" his own virtual text. And there are three features of discourse that seem to me to be crucial in this enlistment process.

The first is the triggering of *presupposition,* the creation of implicit rather than explicit meanings. For with explicitness, the reader's degrees of interpretive freedom are annulled. Examples abound, but Primo Levi's recent *The Periodic Table* provides a particularly striking case. His subtle setting forth of the properties of a particular element in each "story"—argon, hydrogen, zinc, and so on—provide a presuppositional background in terms of which the stories may be "interpreted." How the presuppositional background triggers interpretation is a matter I shall come to shortly.

The second is what I shall call *subjectification:* the depiction of reality not through an omniscient eye that views a timeless reality, but through the filter of the consciousness of protagonists in the story. Joyce, in the stories of *Dubliners*, rarely even hints at how the world really *is*. We see only the realities of the characters themselves—leaving us like the prisoners in Plato's cave, viewing only the shadows of events we can never know directly.

The third is *multiple perspective:* beholding the world not univocally but simultaneously through a set of prisms each of which catches some part of it. Auden's poem on the death of Yeats is a brilliant example: the poet's death is seen in the instruments of winter airports, on the floor of the Bourse, in the sickroom, in the "guts of the living." Roland Barthes argues in *S/Z* that without multiple codes of meaning a story is merely "readerly," not "writerly."

There are doubtless other means by which discourse keeps meaning open or "performable" by the reader—metaphor among them. But the three mentioned suffice for illustration. Together they succeed in *subjunctivizing reality,* which is my way of rendering what Iser means by a narrative speech act. I take my meaning of "subjunctive" from the second one offered by the *OED*: "Designating a mood (L. *modus subjunctivus*) the forms of which are employed to denote an action or state as conceived (and not as a fact) and therefore used to express a wish, command, exhortation, or a contingent, hypothetical, or prospective event." To be in the subjunctive mode is, then, to be trafficking in human possibilities rather than in settled certainties. An "achieved" or "uptaken" narrative speech act, then, produces a subjunctive world. When I use the term *subjunctivize,* I shall mean it in this sense. What then can we say in any technical way about the means whereby discourse portrays a "subjunctive reality"? For surely that is the key to the issue of discourse in great fiction. Let me turn to some of the more systematic ways in which this is accomplished.

Begin with the familiar case of speech acts and Paul Grice's extension of the idea to what he calls the Cooperative Principle governing ordinary conversation. He proposes maxims of quantity (saying only as much as is necessary), of quality (saying only the truth, and saying it with perspicuousness), and of relevance (saying only what is to the point). However needed such maxims may be for regulating conversational cooperation, in fact they are guides to banality: to be brief, perspicuous, truthful, and relevant is to be drab and literal. But the existence of such maxims (however implicit our awareness of them), Grice argues, provides us with the means of violating them for purposes of *meaning more than we say* or for meaning something other than what we say (as in irony, for example) or for meaning less than we say. To mean in this way, by the use of such intended violations or "conversational implicatures," is to create gaps and to recruit presuppositions to fill them. As in

Where's Jack?
Well, I saw a yellow VW outside Susan's.

The reader-hearer, if he is to stay on the narrative scene, must fill in, and under the circumstances he is made complicitous with the characters in the exchange. Why doesn't the respondent say outright (perspicuously) that Jack is visiting Susan? Is it an illicit visit? Is Jack "going the rounds"? Cookbooks on story writing urge the use of implicatures to increase "narrative tension," and they can easily lose their effect when overused. Yet they provide the means for the kind of indirect talk that forces "meaning performance" upon the reader.

Presupposition is an ancient and complex topic in logic and linguistics, and one that deserves closer study by the student of narrative. A presupposition, formally defined, is an implied proposition whose force remains invariant whether the explicit proposition in which it is embedded is true or false. Their nature and operations have been set forth brilliantly by Stephen Levinson, by L. Karttunen and Richard Peters, and by Gerald Gazdar, and their discussions of presuppositional triggers, filters, plugs, and holes are richly suggestive for literary text analysis. They deal with what are called "heritage expressions" and with how a presupposition is built up over discourse in order to project itself into later statements. Triggers effect such projection. Four simple examples will serve to illustrate their manner of operating.

Trigger	Presupposition
Definite descriptions:	
John saw/didn't see the chimera.	There exists a chimera.
Factive verbs:	
John realized/didn't realize he was broke.	John was broke.
Implicative verbs:	
John managed/didn't manage to open the door.	John tried to open the door.
Iteratives:	
You can't get buggy whips anymore.	You used to be able to get buggy whips.

There are many other triggers. I think it is plain (though the details are not easy) that triggering presuppositions, like intentionally violating conversational maxims, provides a powerful way of "meaning more than you are saying," or going beyond surface text, or packing the text with meaning for narrative purposes.

The use of presupposition is greatly facilitated by an informal "contract" that governs language exchanges. As Dan Sperber and Deirdre Wilson have noted, we characteristically assume that what somebody says *must* make sense, and we will, when in doubt about *what* sense it makes, search for or invent an interpretation of the utterance to give it sense. Example on a London street (after Sperber and Wilson):

> Will you buy a raffle ticket for the Royal Naval Lifeboat Institution?
> No thanks, I spend summers near Manchester.
> Ah yes, of course.

Obviously, you cannot press a reader (or a listener) to make endless interpretations of your obscure remarks. But you can go a surprisingly long way—provided only that you start with something approximating what Joseph Campbell called a "mythologically instructed community." And, in fact, most of the devices and tropes that we use in the telling and writing of stories are not substantively as demanding as the one in Sperber and Wilson's example.

To revert to the beginning discussion of paradigmatic and narrative modes of thought, both of them surely trade on presupposition, if only for the sake of brevity. If the scientist or analytic philosopher or logician should be found to be triggering presuppositions in a covert way, he will become the butt of jokes about making a hard sell rather than letting things speak for themselves. His presuppositions should be unpackable, easily so. The writer of fiction who does *not* use such triggering will simply fail. His story will be "flat."

What of subjectification, the rendering of the world of the story into the consciousness of its protagonists? Freud remarks in "The Poet and the Daydream" that the act of composition is, after all, an act of decomposition: the artist's separation of his own internal cast of characters into the characters of the story or play. The plot then becomes a hypothetical actualization of the reader's own internal "psychodynamics." Freud the psychologist thought, of course, that this was achieved unconsciously, and Milosz the poet agrees:

In the very essence of poetry there is something indecent:
A thing is brought forth that we didn't know we had in us,
So we blink our eyes, as if a tiger had sprung out
And stood in the light, lashing his tail.

Freud had it in mind that the "internal drama made external" aids the reader to identify not only with characters but with the human plights in which they find themselves. But this kind of theorizing does not help us much in our understanding of discourse. Is there something more precise that can be said about the language by which subjective landscapes and multiple perspectives are evoked in stories? For that is the issue I am addressing—how is reality rendered subjunctive by language?

An idea of Todorov's serves well as a point of departure. The argument runs somewhat as follows—I say "somewhat" because I am adding some elaborations that are not part of his analysis. Suppose one posits first a "way of saying" that is as simple, expository, and nonsubjunctive as possible: *x commits a crime*. In effect it depicts a "product" or event. It asserts. Todorov proposes that there are six simple transformations that transform the action of the verb from being a fait accompli to being psychologically in process, and as such contingent or subjunctive in our sense. His six simple transformations are as follows:

Mode. Modality, literally a modal auxiliary for the verb, subjectifies the action: *must, might, could, would,* and so on. Modals are ordinarily classified as epistemic and deontic, the first having to do with matters of what could or must be, the second with value obligations: *x must commit a crime* and *x should commit a crime*. And within each class there is a further subdivision between necessity and contingency: *x must commit a crime* and *x might commit a crime,* for example, both of which are "perspectival" triggers. Modal transformations also have the effect of implying a context for an act: x must or x should for some reason, implied but not stated, do what the verb requires.

Intention. Here, the act is directly embedded in its intention: *x plans to commit a crime* (or *hopes to, intends to,* and so on).

Result is a transformation—as in *x succeeds in committing a crime*—whose effect is both to presuppose intent and to raise but leave open the question of how it all came about.

Manner—as in *x is keen to commit a crime*—subjectifies the act and creates an attitude that modifies the action's intention.

Aspect refers to a form of time marking that is related not to an abstract time marker like tense but to the progress of the task in which the action is occurring: for example, *x is beginning to commit a crime* (*is in the midst of,* and so on). Paul Ricoeur's *Time and Narrative* contains an interesting discussion of the way the abstract emptiness of time, defined by tense, must be embodied in a concrete and progressing activity in order for it to constitute narrative time. Aspect transformations are probably the most direct way of providing or evoking such concreteness.

Status—as in *x is not committing a crime*—is a transformation that opens the possibility that there was a wish to, a set of circumstances that, a possibility that, an accusation that could have led to a crime. Negation is a powerful trigger of presuppositions about the possible. "I do not commit crimes" opens a world of alternative perspectives.

Todorov also proposes a half-dozen complex transformations that, in effect, alter a sentence by adding to it a verb phrase that modifies the original or main verb phrase. All of his complex verb phrases have the function of adding "factivity" to the original—that is, a state of mental activity to accompany the main verb phrase. They place the activity in a landscape of consciousness. They are:

Appearance:	x pretends he has committed a crime
Knowledge:	x learns y has committed . . .
Supposition:	x foresees he will commit . . .
Description:	x reports he has committed . . .
Subjectification:	x thinks he has committed . . .
Attitude:	x enjoys committing . . .

To put it in Todorov's words, such a transformation, simple or complex, "permits discourse to acquire a meaning without this meaning becoming pure information." I assume that "pure information" means for him a form of exposition that minimizes presupposition, that keeps the reader from going too far beyond the information given. The use of such transformations, on the other hand, should thicken the connective web that holds a narrative together in its depiction of both action and consciousness.

Can Todorov's system of transformations distinguish good narrative from, say, good exposition? Our research group tried it, comparing one of the stories in Joyce's *Dubliners* with a piece of fine expository writing by the anthropologist Martha Weigel. "Clay" was our story—one on which we had been working intensively. It is a story laced with ritual—Maria laying out the barmbrack for the other girls at the laundry, her tram ride from Ballsbridge to the Pillar and then to Drumcondra, the All Hallows' Eve party and its ritual game of blind man's bluff. This inspired the choice, for comparison, of an expository text to which the same analysis could be applied and that dealt with ritual action. Martha Weigel is an anthropologist and a writer of considerable grace. Her subject is the Southwest and her specialty is the Penitentes, about whom she has written an acclaimed book, *Brothers of Light, Brothers of Blood*. It contains a chapter on rituals. That chapter was our choice.

Gwyneth Lewis and I set out to compare Joyce's "Clay" (113 sentences long) with Weigel's chapter on Penitente rituals—at least its first 113 sentences. The results of the trial run, though they may not be typical of anything save these two pieces, were so striking that I may be forgiven for reporting them here. Consider, for example, the number of Todorovian transformations per 100 sentences of text in the Joyce story and in Weigel's exposition:

Todorovian transformation	Joyce's "Clay"	Weigel's "Rituals"
Simple	117.5	34.6
Complex	84.9	16.0
Total	202.4	50.6

Or, in barest summary, the story contains on average two transformations per sentence; the anthropological account, only one every other sentence.

This, admittedly, is the most grossly unadorned word counting—however much it may be inspired by an hypothesis about how subjunctivizing is achieved. It tells nothing about the contexts in which these transformations are used or about the uses to which they are put. Why do one in three of Joyce's sentences contain transformations of manner, while only one in ten of Martha Weigel's do? Or why are a quarter of Joyce's constructions timed by aspect, while only one in fifty of Weigel's are? A more subtle analysis is for the future.

Rather, I want to say something about "reader response" to the

Joyce story. In our research, we ask our readers to tell us back the story in their own words: to create, so to speak, a virtual text. Again, I can make no claim for the representativeness of what we are finding, but we did subject to analysis the "told back" version of one of our readers, an experienced reader of fiction in his late teens who was reading the story for the first time. He told it back to us a day later. His version of "Clay" was only 24 sentences long (typically shorter than the story), in contrast to Joyce's 113. Compare Joyce and the reader, the numbers standing again for frequency of transformations per 100 sentences.

Todorovian transformation	Joyce's "Clay"	Reader's virtual text
Simple	117.5	235.3
Complex	84.9	91.1
Total	202.4	326.4

Is the reader picking up the subjunctivized speech of the story? Well, there are twice as many simple transformations in the reader's "story" as in Joyce's, and at least as many complex ones as Joyce used. Our reader is plainly resonating to the story and to its discourse as well. Indeed, the two texts, actual and virtual, even agree closely in terms of the frequency ranking of the transformations used. The simple transformations first:

Todorovian transformation	Joyce's "Clay"	Rank	Reader's virtual text	Rank
Manner	33.6	1	83.0	1
Aspect	24.7	2	38.0	3.5
Status	23.8	3	50.0	2
Mode	18.6	4	38.0	3.5
Result	10.6	5	25.0	5
Intention	6.2	6	1.3	6

And the match in the complex transformation was just as close:

Todorovian transformation	Joyce's "Clay"	Rank	Reader's virtual text	Rank
Description	41.6	1	46.0	1
Subjectification	17.7	2	13.8	2

Todorovian transformation	Joyce's "Clay"	Rank	Reader's virtual text	Rank
Attitude	11.5	3	8.0	4.5
Knowledge	9.7	4	11.3	3
Appearance	2.6	5	8.0	4.5
Supposition	1.8	6	4.0	6

What is vividly interesting is that our young reader provided us with a virtual text that, I think, Joyce would not have minded. (It is to be found in the Appendix, placed side-by-side with Joyce's story.) One does not want to make too much of this particular concordance between the "retell" discourse of a reader and the text of a story. But the "results" of this first experiment do suggest some hypotheses. The first is that the "mood"—the *modus subjunctivus*—of the story is preserved in the reading, as well as the substance of the story itself, in the sense both of fabula and sjuzet. There are transformations, to be sure, and (as one can see by comparing the reader's story with Joyce's in the Appendix) these are principally in the form of deletions. Doubtless these deletions serve to "sharpen, level, and assimilate" elements of the story (to use Sir Frederic Bartlett's terms from his classic, *Remembering*). In the retelling, turn-of-the-century Dublin seems a bit more like the New York of today; the episode with the military-looking gentleman on the tram is forefronted in the virtual text more than in the actual one; the doings in the laundry are somewhat flattened.

But perhaps the most interesting qualitative transformation in the retelling is the reader's management of subjunctivity. At first, he tells the story in a way suggesting omniscience about what was happening. This is then modified by peppering the account with "he says" and "he said," where "he" is the author. Then subjunctivizing language begins to take over the virtual text. The reader now says of Maria that "she is going to x," "she wants to x," "she remembers when x," "she thinks what else she wants to x," "she's forced to x," "she becomes used to (accustomed to) x." Or "they start being merry," or "Maria said to Joe that he should make up with his brother Alfy," or "Maria says she's sorry." Or, to take a striking instance of mood preservation, "and Joe says, you know, since its such a nice night I won't get angry about it, but you know, he doesn't; he's not really happy that she brought it up." The subjective landscape is richly constructed in the virtual text, though untransformed "matters of fact" are interspersed ("she goes there and gives the kids their little penny cakes") but only enough to keep a line of action going concurrently with the subjective line.

We also asked our reader a good many questions after he had told back the story so that we might dig a little more deeply into his interpretive activity. For the analysis of virtual text (the "retelling") is only one way of finding out what a story like "Clay" means to a reader. Asked about what had particularly struck him in the story, he picks up the witch theme: "her nose nearly touched her chin." He wonders whether her witchlike appearance clashes with the almost saintly quality she is pictured as possessing. Then he asks, does *she think* she is saintly while others are really sorry for her.

His search for a timeless fabula has begun: "I did kind of get like some kind of evil coming from her . . . even though she was so nice to everybody that she had some hidden evil building up in her, or something." And then, "like artificially nice, almost, like she had no real enemies, she had, you know, she was just nice to everybody, and she wanted everybody, you know, to be nice to her and respect her, which is what she got. But there was that, that, it is not possible for a human to be like that. You know, except, you know, we only saw part of her; we don't know what the other part of her is like." And later he adds, "I was almost happy that he (the old man on the bus), that he had stolen her plum cake, because it's almost like never . . . she was so naive that she'd never experienced anything like that, and I was happy that she had at least had some negative experience, 'cause not everything was always just, you know, hunky-dory and everything. Bad things do happen, when you're so trusting of everybody."

From this interpretation, he then raises a series of questions about symbolism, such as why were they "celebrating Halloween in that ritual, Christmas-like way?" Is it a story about the fall of innocence? He finally decides that it is.

Iser remarks in *The Act of Reading* that readers have both a *strategy* and a *repertoire* that they bring to bear on a text. This reader's principal strategy seemed to consist in trying to reconcile the "stuff" of the story with his repertoire of conceptions about human plights—his collection of possible fabulae. He says early on in so many words that he is "not sure what the story is trying to tell us" but admits that he is caught up in it. His interpretation of "Clay" as a story about "the cost of innocence protected by self-deception" is, so to speak, his personal thumbprint imposed on the story; but it is not entirely idiosyncratic. To begin with, it is not a culturally atypical interpretation (we know from other readers), particularly for a literate New York boy in his late teens. Nor does it do violence to the text: if we had asked other readers to "rate" the cultural appropriateness of his interpretation (which we are now doing in our research in progress), it would have been rated well. As for capturing the author's intent, what can one say? If it were possible to call up the shade of Joyce, he would doubtless turn the question into a pun for Finnegan's wake!

Obviously, it will always be a moot question whether and how well a reader's interpretation "maps" on an actual story, does justice to the writer's intention in telling the story, or conforms to the repertory of a culture. But in any case, the author's act of creating a narrative of a particular kind and in a particular form is not to evoke a standard reaction but to recruit whatever is most appropriate and emotionally lively in the reader's repertory. So "great" storytelling, inevitably, is about compelling human plights that are "accessible" to readers. But at the same time, the plights must be set forth with sufficient subjunctivity to allow them to be *rewritten* by the reader, rewritten so as to allow play for the reader's imagination. One cannot hope to "explain" the processes involved in such rewriting in any but an interpretive way, surely no more precisely, say, than an anthropologist "explains" what the Balinese cockfight means to those who bet on it (to take an example from Clifford Geertz's classic paper on that subject). All that one can hope for is to interpret a reader's interpretation in as detailed and rich a way as psychologically possible.

In the end, one is asking how a reader makes a strange text his own. On this point, there is an instructive exchange between Marco Polo and Kublai Khan in Italo Calvino's *Invisible Cities*. It begins when Marco says:

> "Sire, now I have told you about all the cities I know."
> "There is still one of which you never speak."
> Marco Polo bowed his head.
> "Venice," the Khan said.
> Marco smiled. "What else do you believe I have been talking to you about?"

The emperor did not turn a hair. "And yet I have never heard you mention that name."

And Polo said: "Every time I describe a city I am saying something about Venice."

"When I ask about other cities I want to hear about them. And about Venice, when I ask you about Venice."

"To distinguish the other cities' qualities, I must speak of a first city that remains implicit. For me it is Venice."

Yet, there is something more than assimilating strange tales into the familiar dramas of our own lives, even more than transmuting our own dramas in the process. It is not just strange tales and familiar dramas that are implicated, but something at a level of interpretation beyond story. It is that form of timeless meaning which the story "contains" or instantiates though it is not "in" the story: it is the gist, the plight, perhaps what the Russian Formalists called the *fabula*. There is another exchange between Marco and Kublai that begins to catch the sense of it, of this meaning beyond the details. Marco describes a bridge stone by stone.

"But which is the stone that supports the bridge?" Kublai Khan asks.

"The bridge is not supported by one stone or another," Marco answers, "but by the line of the arch that they form."

Kublai Khan remains silent, reflecting. Then he adds: "Why do you speak to me of the stones? It is only the arch that matters to me."

Polo answers: "Without stones there is no arch."

But still, it is not quite the arch. It is, rather, what arches are *for* in all the senses in which an arch is for something—for their beautiful form, for the chasms they safely bridge, for coming out on the other side of crossings, for a chance to see oneself reflected upside down yet right side up. So a reader goes from stones to arches to the significance of arches is some broader reality—goes back and forth between them in attempting finally to construct a sense of the story, its form, its meaning.

As our readers read, as they begin to construct a virtual text of their own, it is as if they were embarking on a journey without maps—and yet, they possess a stock of maps that *might* give hints, and besides, they know a lot about journeys and about mapmaking. First impressions of the new terrain are, of course, based on older journeys already taken. In time, the new journey becomes a thing in itself, however much its initial shape was borrowed from the past. The virtual text becomes a story of its own, its very strangeness only a contrast with the reader's sense of the ordinary. The fictional landscape, finally, must be given a "reality" of its own—the ontological step. It is then that the reader asks that crucial interpretive question, "What's it all about?" But what "it" is, of course, is not the actual text—however great its literary power—but the text that the reader has constructed under its sway. And that is why the actual text needs the subjunctivity that makes it possible for a reader to create a world of his own. Like Barthes, I believe that the writer's greatest gift to a reader is to help him become a writer.

If I have, then, made much of the contingent and subjunctive not so much in storytelling as in story comprehending, it is because the narrative mode leads to conclusions not about certainties in an aboriginal world, but about the varying perspectives that can be constructed to make experience comprehensible. Beyond Barthes, I believe that the *great* writer's gift to a reader is to make him a *better* writer.

❧

Perhaps the greatest feat in the history of narrative art was the leap from the folktale to the psychological novel that places the engine of action in the characters rather than in the plot. What makes "Clay" a powerful story is not events, but Maria. Without her, the paltry events of the story (and even these are seen only through the eyes of the protagonists) would make no sense. As it is, they are vivid little epiphanies of ordinariness—her ordinariness, and through her, our ordinariness.

What is at the heart of the psychological story is the notion of a "character" or a "cast of characters." Our young reader of "Clay" ends with "It's actually a depressing story when you get down to it . . . like what's it all about for Maria, like what's it all leading to? She works, she's an old lady . . . she's done you know probably nothing." He has converted the story into a tale of character—character and circumstance.

Character is an extraordinarily elusive literary idea. Perhaps it is elusive for reasons beyond the literary. For even in "real life," it is always a moot question whether the actions of persons should be attributed to circumstances or to their "enduring dispositions"—their character. Aristotle in the *Poetics* conveniently distinguishes between "agent" (*pratton*) and "character" (*ethos*), the former being a figure in a drama whose actions merely fit the requirements of the plot, and no more, while the latter has traits beyond those required. But this is by no means clear for, as Ricoeur reminds us in *Time and Narrative*, Aristotle's idea of *mimesis* includes the notion that drama reflects "character in action" and action surely involves plot and its setting. Besides, can there ever be a figure in a drama who does *just* what is required by the plot without giving some inkling of what he or she would be like in more general terms? As Seymour Chatman puts it, "If one trait is assigned to an action, why isn't the floodgate thereby opened?" Ask a reader whether he would be comfortable buying a second-hand car from a "false hero" in a Proppian fairytale, or what kind of relationship that false hero might have had with his father. It will soon be plain, as Solomon Asch demonstrated a generation ago, that character (or perhaps we should call it *apparent* character) is not a bundle of autonomous traits but an organized conception, however much we may construct it from such scraps and clues as we can find.

Asch made his point by demonstrating how differently the trait *intelligent* was interpreted depending on whether the character to whom it was attributed was also described as *cold* or as *warm*. In the first case, intelligent meant "crafty," while in the second it was taken to mean "wise." Apparent character is perceived as a *Gestalt,* not as a list of traits that account for particular actions. And the Gestalt seems to be constructed according to some sort of theory about how people are. For example, they have some sort of core characteristic that directs their behavior from within. But if the person in question behaves in a way that violates that core characteristic, we easily explain it away by invoking circumstances. My colleague Henri Zukier and I tried out some typical college-aged readers on a variant of the Asch experiment. To begin with, we gave them a short list of consistent trait names characterizing an imaginary person, like *spiritual, introverted, religious,* to which they would respond by describing him as "a saintly kind of person." Then we added to the list *practical* and *money-minded.* One subject: "Sure. A good man, but he's probably in one of those cut-throat businesses." Another: "I've known them like that—like one of those Amish or Mennonite farmers where I grew up, good in his own group and drives a hard bargain outside." (Interestingly enough, when subjects begin telling about "circumstances," their language quickly becomes drenched in Todorov transformations.)

The inseparability of character, setting, and action must be deeply rooted in the nature of narrative thought. It is only with difficulty that we can conceive of each of them in isolation. There are different ways of combining the three in constructing the *dramatis personae* of fiction (or of life, for that matter). And those constructions are by no means arbitrary. They reflect psychological processes such as those noted by Asch and other psychologists. They also reflect our beliefs about how people fit into society. The alternate ways in which we can construe people, moreover, often run into conflict with each other, and the conflict leaves us puzzled. Indeed, the act of construing another person is almost inevitably problematic. For all that, the choice of one construal rather than another virtually always has real consequences for how we deal with others. Our construal of character, indeed, is our first and perhaps most important step in dealing with another. It is this that makes the very act of interpreting a person—whether in fiction or in life—inherently dramatic. It is what makes the narrative of character so much more subjunctive than the folktale or the myth.

How characterize the different ways in which we construe "personhood" in literature? We could, of course, adopt the character types offered by theories of "personality" from Galen to Freud and Jung, and see whether readers of fiction use the same categories. But that is too specialized. We already know that even the most ordinary readers go beyond mere character depictions to consideration of circumstance and setting. We need, rather, a "morphology" of persons that captures common sense, that takes into account the range of concerns I have mentioned. Then we can explore how in fact readers fit character, plot, and action together in making the virtual text.

Amélie Rorty offers an analysis that, I think, is to the point. It distinguishes characters, figures, persons, selves, and individuals. She begins with a sketch: "*Characters* are delineated; their traits are sketched; they are not presumed to be strictly unified. They appear in novels by Dickens, not those by Kafka. *Figures* appear in cautionary tales, exemplary novels and hagiography. They present narratives of types of lives to be imitated. *Selves* are possessors of their properties. *Individuals* are centers of integrity; their rights are inalienable." The use of these variant construals is, for Rorty, fraught with human consequences: "we are different entities as we conceive ourselves enlightened by these various views. Our powers of action are different, our relations to one another, our properties and proprieties, our characteristic successes or defeats, our conception of society's proper strictures and freedoms will vary with our conceptions of ourselves as characters, persons, selves, individuals."

Let me very briefly sketch Rorty's views and then return more directly to the general point. She sees *characters* as evolved from their origin in the Greek concept of the hero. The hero is known by his deeds. "As the hero's distance from the gods increases, his heroism comes to be exemplified in his character rather than in the sheer glory of his action." Characters do not have identity crises, since there is no presupposition about their unity; but disharmony among their characteristics breeds trouble—in their action, not in their selfhood. To know what sort of character a person is is to know the circumstances that suit him best, for not all characters are suited to the same life. A character's tragedy is to be in circumstances where his disposition is no longer needed, no longer suited. "Characters in time of great social change . . . are likely to be tragic." And then, "In fiction, characters are dear to us because they are predictable, because they entitle us to the superiority of gods who can lovingly foresee and thus more readily forgive what is fixed."

Figures "are defined by their place in an unfolding drama; they are not assigned roles because of their traits, but rather have the traits of their prototypes in myth or sacred script. Figures are characters writ large, become figureheads . . . Both their roles and their traits emerge from their place in an ancient narrative. The narration, the plot, comes first . . ." Whatever else figures are doing, they are filling their roles. A confidante may have gone to buy fish, but her real role is the sharing of confidences. "A figure is neither formed by nor owns experience." They are Mary or Martha, Peter or Paul, Che Guevara or Paul Bunyan.

The idea of *persons,* Rorty proposes, comes from two sources: the *dramatis personae* of the stage, and the law. "A person's roles and his place in the narrative devolve from the choices that place him in a structural system, related to others." Central to it is the idea of a unified center of action and choice—the unit of both legal and theological responsibility. Interest in persons, then, centers upon locating liability.

The scope of a person lies in his powers to affect those around him, a scope for which he bears responsibility.

When we conceive of persons exclusively as sources of responsibility, we think of them as souls or minds, engaged with *res cogitans*. When we think of them as possessing rights and powers, we think of them as *selves*. "When a society has changed so that individuals acquire their rights by virtue of their powers, rather than having their powers defined by their rights, the concept of person has been transformed to a concept of self." Jane Austen describes a world of persons on the verge of becoming selves, Trollope one that has already become a world of selves, one in which the property required for stature is no longer land but an assured income due one by virtue of one's qualities.

Finally, *individuality,* born out of the corruption in societies of selves: "It begins with conscience and ends with consciousness." At its core is a contrast of individual *versus* society: "an individual transcends and resists what is binding and oppressive in society and does so from an original natural position . . . The rights of persons are formulated *in* society, while the rights of individuals are demanded *of* society." And so Molloy and Malone, the zaniness of the individual soldier in the midst of an insane war, rip-off as the redistribution of property.

Each is a mode of interpreting as well as a mode of depiction, and in both, the lines are not clear. Depictions achieve drama by embodying a conflict: is Leggatt in *The Secret Sharer* a "figure" or an "individual" in Rorty's sense? And as writers alter their "presentation" of personhood—from the figures of Homer to the characters of Euripides, from Jane Austen's persons to Trollope's selves, from Conrad's selves to Beckett's individuals—so too readers change in the approach to personhood. In life, is it crusading senator or macho lover of Marilyn Monroe, a teenage offender in the light of love or the light of justice, which Roger Casement, which of the two Parnells. In literature, is Roth's Zuckerman a character who searches for the setting that will uncork his gifts, the figure in a morality drama, or the individual in revolt?

Lionel Trilling, reviewing David Riesman's *The Lonely Crowd,* conjectured whether modern sociology was coming to take the place of the novel as a window on the lives of those who live in "other" social classes. But that cannot be right. For the anomaly of personhood—its consequential alternativeness—cannot be caught save through the vehicle of narrative. And it is this alternativeness—this inherent restlessness in deciding on the right depiction of personhood—that gives the novel of character, the psychological novel, its force, its subjunctivity, and its power to disturb.

❧

One final point and I am done. It is about narrative and history. In a recent book on historiography, Dale Porter raises some extremely interesting questions about the strengths and shortcomings of narrative history. I do not want to evaluate his arguments, but to comment on one point that recurs in his account (as it has in earlier accounts by Bryce Gallie and by Isaiah Berlin). There is an assumption, implicit to be sure, that a narrative account leaves one open to "errors" that are departures from an aboriginal reality that is better discerned by a more systematic, "logico-scientific" method. After all, what we know, the *annales,* so to speak, is that on Christmas Day at the Vatican in the year 800, Pope Leo III crowned Charlemagne Emperor of the Holy Roman Empire. When an historian of the stature of Louis Halphen sets these bare "facts" into a web of imperial and papal intentions and of changing "world views," does he risk errors that are more egregious and fanciful than, say, the errors in wait for a sober economic historian who eschews narratives? That one does something more verifiable than the other, few would doubt. Trade and commerce, the flow of capital, and so on are documentable in a way that motives and a growing "sense of Europeanness" are not. So should Halphen's account be treated as a form of fiction (or "faction") or as fictionalized history?

The economist Robert Heilbroner once remarked that when forecasts based on economic theory fail, he and his colleagues take to telling stories—about Japanese managers, about the Zurich "snake," about the Bank of England's "determination" to keep sterling from falling. There is a curious anomaly here: businessmen and bankers today (like men of affairs of all ages) guide their decisions by just such stories—even when a workable theory is available. These narratives, once acted out, "make" events and "make" history. They contribute to the reality of the participants. For an economist (or an economic historian) to ignore them, even on grounds that "general economic forces" shape the world of economics, would be to don blinders. Can anyone say a priori that history is completely independent of what goes on in the minds of its participants? Narratives may be the last resort of economic theorists. But they are probably the life stuff of those whose behavior they study.

So we embellish our hard-core *annales,* convert them into *chroniques* and finally into narrative *histoires* (to borrow Hayden White's way of putting it). And thereby we constitute the psychological and cultural reality in which the participants in history actually live. In the end, then, the narrative and the paradigmatic come to live side by side. All the more reason for us to move toward an understanding of what is involved in telling and understanding great stories, and how it is that stories create a reality of their own—in life as in art.

3

Possible Castles

Science and the humanities—an ancient topic, even a tired one. Like the faint lavender of old closets whose family gowns and dress suits and old uniforms are too interesting to throw away yet plainly not suited to modern living, brought out only on special occasions. When the ancient topic was trotted out, it was either to display the eternally warm relevance of the humanities (in contrast to the cold heartlessness of science) or to vaunt the dispassionate rationality of science (in contrast to the partisan muddle-headed humanities). The old tub thumpings are no longer so convincing.

Our once tired topic seems to have come awake again. Once technical issues in philosophy—constructivism, theories of meaning, the status of scientific concepts—have brought the sleepwalker alive. Given that mind itself constructs scientific theories, historical explanations, or metaphoric renderings of experience by related forms of world making, the old discussion has shifted from the *products* of scientific and humanistic inquiry to the *processes* of inquiry themselves. The body of scientifically verifiable objective knowledge is no longer to be so simply arrayed against the soft, suppositious, and subjective products of the humanities. Their procedures now occupy us.

Both science and the humanities have come to be appreciated as artful figments of men's minds, as creations produced by different uses of mind. The world of Milton's "Paradise Lost" and the world of Newton's *Principia* exist not only in the minds of men; each has an existence in an "objective world" of culture—what the philosopher

Karl Popper calls World Three. They are both, in the sense of modern modal logic, collections of *possible worlds*. Neither threatens the other with falsification; neither is derivable from the other save in terms of remote heritage: what the logician K. J. J. Hintikka calls *heir lines* between possible worlds. Falsification, indeed, becomes a much more interesting process under this dispensation. In the new, more powerful modal logic, we ask of a proposition not whether it is true or false, but in what kind of possible world it would be true. It is the case, moreover, that if it can be demonstrated to be true in *all* conceivable possible worlds, then it is almost certainly a truth that derives from the nature of language rather than from the world—in the sense that the statement "a bachelor is an unmarried male" may be true in all possible worlds.

This brings me to the title of this chapter, "Possible Castles." In 1976 Gordon Mills published a thoughtful book entitled *Hamlet's Castle*. It begins with an intriguing epigraph:

> In the Spring of the year 1924 the young German physicist Werner Heisenberg went on a walking tour with the great Niels Bohr in Denmark, Bohr's homeland. The following is Heisenberg's account of what Bohr said when they came to Kronberg Castle.
>
>> Isn't it strange how this castle changes as soon as one imagines that Hamlet lived here. As scientists we believe that a castle consists only of stones, and admire the way the architect put them together. The stone, the green roof with its patina, the wood carvings in the church, constitute the whole castle. None of this should be changed by the fact that Hamlet lived here, and yet it is changed completely. Suddenly the walls and the ramparts speak a different language. The courtyard becomes an entire world, a dark corner reminds us of the darkness of the human soul, we hear Hamlet's "To be or not to be." Yet all we really know about Hamlet is that his name appears in a thirteenth-century chronicle. No one can prove that he really lived here. But everyone knows the questions Shakespeare had him ask, the human depths he was made to reveal, and so he too had to be found a place on earth, here in Kronberg.

I want to explore some of the ways in which we create products of mind, how we come to experience them as real, and how we manage to build them into the corpus of a culture as science, literature, history, whatever. In the end, I hope I will be able to make the strong case that it is far more important, for appreciating the human condition, to understand the ways human beings construct their worlds (and their castles) than it is to establish the ontological status of the products of these processes. For my central ontological conviction is that there is no "aboriginal" reality against which one can compare a possible world in order to establish some form of correspondence between it and the real world—a conviction I shall discuss in a later chapter on the work of Nelson Goodman (Chapter 7).

❧

Let me begin with the topic of surprise. Surprise is an extraordinarily useful phenomenon to students of mind, for it allows us to probe what people take for granted. It provides a window on presupposition: surprise is a response to violated presupposition. Presupposition, of course, is what is taken for granted, what is expected to be the case. Our central nervous system seems to have evolved in a way that specializes our senses to deal differently with expected and with unexpected versions of the world. Unexpected versions (unexpected in the sense that such versions violate the neural "models of the world" stored in the brain) most often alert the cerebral cortex through discharge of impulses in the so-called ascending reticular system, a tangled skein of fibers that runs in parallel with orderly sensory nerves, both working their way upstream to the upper brain. Yet, this makes the matter sound too static. Better to say that the nervous system stores models of the world that, so to speak, spin a little faster than the world goes. If what impinges on us conforms to expectancy, to the predicted state of the model, we may let our attention flag a little, look elsewhere, even go to sleep. Let input violate expectancy, and the system is put on alert. Any input, then, must be conceived of as being made up not only of environmentally produced stimulation but also of accompanying markings of its conformity with or discrepance from what the nervous system is expecting. If all is in conformity, we adapt and may even stop noticing, as we stop noticing the touch sensation produced by our clothes or the lint on the lens of our eyeglasses.

The study of human perception reveals how powerfully constrained our perceptual system is by this deep principle. Thresholds, the amount of time and input necessary for seeing or recognizing an object or event, are closely governed by expectancy. The more expected an event, the more easily it is seen or heard. There is a limit on the amount the system can take in—its channel capacity, said to be 7 ± 2 slots, the Magic Number. You can get a lot of expected information into seven slots, but much less unexpected information. The more unexpected the information, the more processing space it takes up. All this is banal enough, but its implications are anything but that. For it means that perception is to some unspecifiable degree an instrument of the world as we have structured it by our expectancies. Moreover, it is characteristic of complex perceptual processes that they tend where possible to assimilate whatever is seen or heard to what is expected. Leo Postman and I conducted an amusing demonstration experiment many years ago, involving the recognition of tachistoscopically presented playing cards—giving the subject only milliseconds of exposure to our displays and increasing exposure successively. The displays consisted of both normal playing cards and ones in which color and suit were reversed—a red six of clubs, for example. The reversed cards, as one would expect, took much longer to recognize. But more interestingly, our subjects went to extraordinary lengths to "regularize" the reversed cards to make them conform to their canonical pattern. I recall one reporting that our red six of clubs was indeed a six of clubs, but that the illumination inside the tachistoscope was rather pinkish! In fact, what human perceivers do is to take whatever scraps they can extract from the stimulus input, and if these conform to expectancy, to read the rest from the model in their head. The philosopher Thomas Kuhn was sufficiently beguiled by our experiment that he took it as a paradigm of what he came to call paradigms in science.

Can we say anything interesting and succinct about the general properties of the models that we store in our heads that guide our perception, thought, and talk? In the main, they appear to be diverse, rich, local, extraordinarily generative. Some of them seem principally to be based on our stored knowledge of versions of the world we have "encountered." My mental model of how traffic moves in New York or in London is built up of many such encounters. I have developed a feel for what to expect and I usually see what I am looking for, no matter what else I may miss. I use my model to guide my behavior and drive or walk defensively in terms of that model. My defensiveness also regulates what I take up in input. The surprises I encounter are most often generated by others violating the usual or doing something "against the rules."

My local traffic sense is a different model from the one that guides my sailing into a harbor full of shoals, when, as the saying goes, I depend upon my channel sense. But, in some difficult-to-specify way, the two models are related. They constitute a genre of models. The more I reflect upon the two models, the more they seem to become related by a reflective recognition of certain "general principles." These general principles, we would say, seem more formal or abstract, more content-free. Traffic flow and the movements of a flow in a tidal channel come to be seen in terms of where "things"—whether sand or motor vehicles—pile up, where they move easily. My knowledge becomes more hierarchically organized, more like science. I come to appreciate books, like Ascher Shapiro's, on the abstract topic of "flow."

In time I might even find or construct a general mathematical model that characterizes how it is to flow about among obstructions. Occasionally, indeed, such models will grow to be as abstract and embracing as Newton's principle defining gravitational attraction as directly proportional to the mass of each body and inversely proportional to the distance between them. The virtue of such models is that they enable us to keep an enormous amount in mind while paying attention to a minimum of detail. This is the crowning achievement of the kind of model creation that we call "science"—one of the forms of world making.

But I fear I have rendered it too gray and orderly. World making of this type rides from time to time on wild metaphors as well. The history of science is full of them. They are crutches to help us get up the abstract mountain. Once up, we throw them away (even hide them) in favor of a formal, logically consistent theory that (with luck) can be stated in mathematical or near-mathematical terms. The formal models that emerge are shared, carefully guarded against attack, and prescribe ways of life for their users. The metaphors that aided in this achievement are usually forgotten or, if the ascent turns out to be important, are made not part of science but part of the history of science.

We build our models, make our worlds, quite differently for guiding our transactions with other human beings in everyday life. I have just finished a decade of work, studying the beginnings of human interaction between infants and their adult caretakers, trying to discover the theories they build about each other, and particularly how the infants get launched into the use of human language. These interactions soon begin to fall into formats—types of activities in which the partners can predict each other, attribute intentions, and in general assign interpretations to each other's acts and utterances. The formats are plainly theory-bound and girded by presuppositions, for when they are violated the infant is quick to surprise, and even indignation. With experience, our models both specialize and generalize: we develop theories about *kinds* of people, *kinds* of problems, *kinds* of human conditions. The categories and maxims of these "folk theories" are rarely put directly to the test. They are rarely original, and are more likely to come from the folk wisdom of the culture in which we grow up.

As I noted in the preceding chapter, folk theories about the human condition remain embedded in metaphor and in a language that serves the end of narrative. And folk narrative of this kind has as much claim to "reality" as any theory we may construct in psychology by the use of our most astringent scientific methods. Indeed, many thoughtful students of psychology believe that one of the richest sources of data for the construction of an adequate psychology are these very folk theories—a notable example being Fritz Heider. Such a psychology would, of course, be more "interpretive" than positivist, its task being to provide a richer, yet more abstract interpretation of human "theories in action," much as the interpretive cultural anthropologist provides an *explication de texte* of the culture.

This brings us directly to the activities of the humanist—the historian, the literary critic, the philosopher, the interpreter of culture. And, of course, the artist: the poet, the storyteller, the painter, the dramatist, the maker of music.

The artist creates possible worlds through the metaphoric transformation of the ordinary and the conventionally "given." Let me take an example: the devil. In "Paradise Lost," Milton creates an image of the devil that beggars the simplistic notion of him as an agent of evil and unreason. It is comparable in its metaphoric power to Freud's Id metaphor of Unreason. Just as Freud makes unreason wily and even witty in its ways (rather than merely loutish and brutal) by ascribing to it clever slips of the tongue and even forms of wit, so Milton gives the devil a strategy and, indeed, a character. In the poem, Satan has as his aim the creation of doubt. He is opposed to blind faith.

Satan shows his first chagrin on finding Adam and Eve "emparadised in each other's arms." It is not an auspicious posture in which to find those in whom one wishes to create doubt. When Adam then tells Eve that all is hers in the Garden save the forbidden fruit, Satan sees an opening. Too towering the naive faith of this man, who believes that God created him in his own image yet forbids him access to the Tree of Knowledge. Perhaps he can get at the woman. This is not a fiend, not a sniggering tempter. He is a Satan of principles, a devil with a mission. He is against faith. He goes about his business methodically, like Freud's Id. For the reader, issues of good and evil are transformed by such a devil, just as Kronberg is transformed by Hamlet's having lived there. Things as culturally real as faith and reason take on new meanings. We rethink history, reconstrue its Dark Ages and its Renaissance.

❧

On the account I have given, it would seem that science and the humanities start at some convergent origin and diverge in terms of method. But I think this fails to capture one other crucial difference. They may begin at a common origin, but they diverge and specialize with different aims in mind where world making is concerned. Science attempts to make a world that remains invariant across human intentions and human plights. The density of the atmosphere does not, must not alter as a function of one's ennui with the world. On the other hand, the humanist deals principally with the world as it changes with the position and stance of the viewer. Science creates a world that has an "existence" linked to the invariance of things and events across transformations in the life conditions of those who seek to understand—though modern physics has shown that this is true within very constrained limits. The humanities seek to understand the world as it reflects the requirements of living in it. In the jargon of linguistics, a work of literature or of literary criticism achieves universality through context sensitivity, a work of science through context independence. I shall deal later with the meaning of "universality" in these two senses.

Karl Popper is often scorned for characterizing science as principally concerned with falsification. His is a very austere, a very public view of science. In fact, science as reported and codified has no place for accounts of hypothesis *forming*—except insofar as it can be reduced to the process of induction on the one hand or of the hypothetico-deductive method on the other. Journals of science do not give space to rambles through metaphor, to the processes by which we get ideas worth testing—that is, worth falsifying. Yet a great deal of the time of scientists is spent in just such rambling. Let me say now what Niels Bohr told *me*. The idea of complementarity in quantum theory, he said, came to him as he thought of the impossibility of considering his son simultaneously in the light of love and in the light of justice, the son just having voluntarily confessed that he had stolen a pipe from a local shop. His brooding set him to thinking about the vases and the faces in the trick figure-ground pictures: you can see only one at a time. And then the impossibility of thinking simultaneously about the position and the velocity of a particle occurred to him. That tale, we are told, belongs in the history of science, not in science itself.

I think that Popper, nonetheless, is more right than wrong. Falsification is crucial to us for one overwhelming reason. Man, we know, is infinitely capable of belief. Surprising that he has not been described as *Homo credens*. Harold Garfinkel, now a distinguished sociologist, once took a "reading and research" course with me in order to find out what psychologists were up to. He hit on a very interesting experiment. Borrowing a dozen trait names from one of the standard lists, each with a positive and negative pole—like *lazy* and *energetic, honest* and *dishonest*—he selected at random combinations of negatives and positives. He presented these combinations on cards and asked his subjects for a general description of the person being depicted. They could always oblige, no matter how unlikely the combination. None of his subjects *ever* said "This is impossible: there just couldn't be such a person." Now, perhaps there *can* be every kind of person. Or perhaps the better way to say it is that we can create hypotheses that will accommodate virtually anything we encounter.

It is this staggering gift for creating hypotheses that makes Popper's austere view of science more right than wrong—that and the ease with which, by the very selectivity of our senses, our minds, and our language, we accept our hypotheses as right. We have extraordinary faith in one-shot instantiation. Milton's Satan in "Paradise Lost" may have been the forerunner of Karl Popper's falsificationism.

For all that, we know that if we are to appreciate and understand an imaginative story (or an imaginative hypothesis, for that matter) we must "suspend disbelief," accept what we hear for the time being as putatively real, as stipulative. With science, we ask finally for some verification (or some proof against falsification). In the domain of narrative and explication of human action, we ask instead that, upon reflection, the account correspond to some perspective we can imagine or "feel" as right. The one, science, is oriented outward to an external world; the other, inward toward a perspective and a point of view toward the world. They are, in effect, two forms of an illusion of reality—very different forms. But their respective "falsifiability" in Popper's sense does not fully distinguish them.

Rather, I think, we need to examine what it means to say that a constructed world—for example, a novel, a narrative history, a piece of literary or cultural criticism—is matched against our perspective and our point of view. When the painter Manet exclaimed, "Nature is only an hypothesis," he could not have meant it in a Popperian spirit. It was, rather, a battle cry against academic representationalism as the only, or even the good, way to depict nature in painting. It was an invitation to create more, different, and even shocking hypotheses.

For, in effect, the humanities have as their implicit agenda the cultivation of hypotheses, the art of hypothesis generating. It is in hypothesis generating (rather than in hypothesis falsification) that one cultivates multiple perspectives and possible worlds to match the requirements of those perspectives.

To the degree that modern science (or science in any era, regardless of Newton's famous *hypothesis non fingo*) also is involved in hypothesis generating, as well as in hypothesis testing, it is akin to the activities of the humanist and the artist. That much we know from examining the metaphoric crutches with which the good intuitive scientist proceeds up his abstract mountain. But his object is always to convert those dense metaphors into the transparent, frangible hypotheses of science—or into untestable axioms that will generate hypotheses that, with luck, may be tested.

As for art and the humanities, they too are constrained in the kinds of hypotheses they generate, but *not* by constraints of testability in the scientists' sense, and *not* by the search for hypotheses that will be true across a wide range of human perspectives. Rather, the aim (as already noted in the preceding chapters) is that the hypotheses fit different human perspectives and that they be recognizable as "true to conceivable experience": that they have verisimilitude.

Which is not to say that the trade of the humanist is in particulars rather than in universals. For here we must turn to an issue raised at the end of the previous chapter.

Return to Pope Leo III crowning Charlemagne as Holy Roman Emperor at the Vatican on Christmas Day in the year 800, and to Louis Halphen's reconstruction of the "causes" and background of that unique event. If we are to understand it, it will not be by means of a positivist archaeology in which everything particular about it and everything leading up to it are finally dug up, labeled, and collated. However much we dig and delve, there is still an interpretive task. It is a task promoted by rich hypothesis generation, some of the hypotheses obviously being subject to falsifiability. Was Leo the brother of Charlemagne, a nepotism theorist may ask? Well, plainly not. That can be falsified. Was Leo trying to strengthen his alliances to protect the Church against the advance of Arab power? Well, possibly, for that power was still on the rise. And more universally, is it not the case that heads of state always seek to form alliances against impending encroachment? The historian can surely look for congruent evidence in the archives. But we, as readers of Carolingian history, will look for alternative hypotheses—even if we already believe the alliance theory.

For the object of understanding human events is to sense the alternativeness of human possibility. And so there will be no end of interpretations of Charlemagne's ascendance (or Jeanne d'Arc's fall or Cromwell's rise and fall)—and not only by historians, but by novelists, poets, playwrights, and even philosophers.

❧

So in the end, what shall we say about the relation of the sciences and the humanities? What shall we say about Lucretius's *De rerum natura*? An evocative poem but bad physics? If hypothesis *making* is part of physics, well, Lucretius's poem is full of interesting, original, and eventually falsifiable hypotheses. Its evocativeness as a poem comes precisely from the rich bed of metaphor from which it grows, so that it is readable to us today as a metaphoric perspective on the world of nature.

Aristotle in the *Poetics* (II.9) puts the conclusion well: "The poet's function is to describe, not the thing that has happened, but a kind of thing that might happen, i.e., what is possible as being probable or necessary . . . And if he should come to take a subject from actual history, he is none the less a poet for that; since some historic occurrences may very well be in the probably once possible order of things: and it is in that aspect of them that he is their poet."

Perhaps this is why tyrants so hate and fear poets and novelists and, yes, historians. Even more than they fear and hate scientists, who, though they create possible worlds, leave no place in them for possible alternative personal perspectives on those worlds.

Part Two

Language and Reality

4

The Transactional Self

If you engage for long in the study of how human beings relate to one another, especially through the use of language, you are bound to be struck by the importance of "transactions." This is not an easy word to define. I want to signify those dealings which are premised on a mutual sharing of assumptions and beliefs about how the world is, how mind works, what we are up to, and how communication should proceed. It is an idea captured to some extent by Paul Grice's maxims about how to proceed in conversation, by Deirdre Wilson and Dan Sperber's notion that we always assume that what others have said must make *some* sense, by Hilary Putnam's recognition that we usually assign the right level of ignorance or cleverness to our interlocutors. Beyond these specifics, there remains a shady but important area of sharing—Colwyn Trevarthen calls it "intersubjectivity"—that makes the philosopher's query about how we know Other Minds seem more practical than the philosopher ever intended it to be.

One knows intuitively as a psychologist (or simply as a human being) that the easy access we have into each other's minds, not so much in the particulars of what we are thinking but in general about what minds are like, cannot be explained away by invoking singular concepts like "empathy." Nor does it seem sufficient to perform a miracle of phenomenology, as did the German philosopher Max Scheler, and subdivide *Einfuhlung* into a half-dozen "feelable" classes. Or to take the route of nineteenth-century psychologists and elevate "sympathy" to the status of an instinct. More typically, the contemporary student of mind will try to unravel the mystery by exploring how we develop this sense of what other minds are about, or by examining its pathologies, as in autistic children and in young schizophrenics. Or he will try to unravel the details of interpersonal knowledge among adults by conducting experiments on facets of this knowledge, as have Fritz Heider and his students. Or, yet another alternative, he will dismiss the issue of intersubjective knowledge as "nothing but" projection, for whatever smug satisfaction that may give him.

I first became caught up in this issue through work I did in collaboration with Renato Tagiuri, and we ended up writing a chapter on "person perception" in one of the standard Handbooks—treating it as a perceptual problem. Along the way to that chapter we did some of those little experiments which are the craft of psychology. We asked people who were parts of small groups or cliques and who knew each other well two very simple questions: who in the group would they (each individual) most like to spend more time with, and who in the group did they think would most like to spend more time with them. I should say at the outset that this is a procedure fraught with statistical problems, particularly if one wants to study the "accuracy" of interpersonal perceptions or to determine whether people's choices are "transparent" to others. But the statistical hurdles can be jumped by using what are called "Monte Carlo procedures," which consist of allocating each person's choices and guesses of others' choices with the aid of a roulette wheel. One can then compare the subjects' real performance with the wheel's allocation of choices and guesses by chance. Yes, on average people are more accurate and more transparent than would be expected by chance—a not very startling finding. They know better than chance who likes them, or to put it inversely, people's preferences are transparent.

But there is something very curious about how people operate in such situations that is not so obvious after all. For one thing, a person who chooses another will (in excess of chance) believe that the other person chooses him back. Or, since the direction of cause is never clear in human affairs, if we *feel* chosen by somebody, we will choose that person in return whether our feeling is correct or not. There is simply a human bias: feeling liked by somebody begets liking him back. To this add the fact that we know better than chance who likes us. Now, is this a matter of "accuracy" or of "vanity"? Are we "victims" of vanity or beneficiaries of our sensitivity? If we bias our Monte Carlo wheels with these same "human" tendencies, they will perform indistinguishably from humans. Does that mean that humans are simply biased robots? Is that a meaningful question, really? It smacks altogether too much of those early Cartesian questions about man as a machine with a human soul added to it, perhaps making its will known through the pineal gland just as we can make "humanness" available to the Monte Carlo robot by rigging the wheel.

The model we had been using seemed wrong—or at least it led us down dead ends where we did not want to travel. What it told us—and it was not trivial—was that shared sensitivities and biases can produce some strikingly social consequences. For one thing, they produce astonishing stability within groups. People act in accordance with their perceptions and their choices, and they reciprocate accordingly. We created a little discussion group of seven members, to discuss "psychology and life" (they were all undergraduates). And we administered our test four or five times over a term. Some interesting things happened to the dyads or pairs that composed that group. Certain patterns virtually disappeared over time or occurred eventually at levels *below* chance. Instances of pairs in which each chose the other with neither feeling chosen in return were gone by the end of the term. So too were cases where both felt chosen by the other but did not choose in return. The transactional process seemed to intensify over time. We left it at that and went off to pursue other matters.

But the problem was to return, and it did so, more than a decade later, when I began a series of studies on growth in human infancy and particularly on the development of human language and its precursors. My first brush with it was in studying the development of exchange games in infancy, when I was struck with how quickly and easily a child, once having mastered the manipulation of objects, could enter into "handing back and forth," handing objects around a circle, exchanging objects for each other. The competence seemed there, as if *ab ovum;* the performance was what needed some smoothing out. Very young children had something clearly in mind about what others had in mind, and organized their actions accordingly. I thought of it as the child achieving mastery of one of the precursors of language use: a sense of mutuality in action.

So too in a second study (which I shall tell about more fully later) in which we were interested in how the child came to manage his attention jointly with others—a prerequisite of linguistic reference. We found that by their first birthday children are already adept at following another's line of regard to search for an object that is engaging their partner's attention. That surely requires a sophisticated conception of a partner's mind.

Yet why should we have been surprised? The child has such conceptions "in mind" in approaching language. Children show virtually no difficulty in mastering pronouns and certain demonstratives, for example, even though these constitute that confusing class of referring expressions called deictic shifters. A deictic shifter is an expression whose meaning one can grasp only through appreciating the interpersonal context in which it is uttered and by whom it is uttered. That is to say, when I use the pronoun *I*, it means me; when my partner uses it, it refers to him. A spatial shifter pair like *here* and *there* poses the same problem: *here* used by me is close to me; *here* used by you is close to you. The shifter ought to be hard to solve for the child, and yet it isn't.

It *ought* to be, that is, if the child were as "self-centered" as he is initially made out to be by current theories of child development. For our current theories (with notable exceptions carried over from the past, like the views of George Herbert Mead) picture the child as starting his career in infancy and continuing it for some years after, locked in his own perspective, unable to take the perspective of another with whom he is in interaction. And, indeed, there are even experimental "demonstrations" to prove the point. But *what* point? Surely not that we can take any perspective of anybody in any plight at any time. We would not have been so slow in achieving the Copernican revolution if that were the case, or in understanding that to the Indians North America must have seemed like *their* homeland. To show that a child (or an adult) cannot, for example, figure out what three mountains he sees before him might look like to somebody viewing them from their "back" sides (to take as our whipping boy one of the classic experiments demonstrating egocentrism), does not mean he cannot take another's perspective into account *in general*.

It is curious, in view of the kinds of considerations I have raised, that psychological theories of development have pictured the young child as so lacking in the skills of transaction. The prevailing view of initial (and slowly waning) egocentrism is, in certain respects, so grossly, almost incongruously wrong and yet so durable, that it deserves to be looked at with care. Then we can get back to the main issue—what it is that readies the child so early for transacting his life with others on the basis of some workable intuitions about Other Minds and, perhaps, about Human Situations as well. The standard view seems to have four principal tenets:

1. *Egocentric perspective.* That initially young children are incapable of taking the perspective of others, have no conception of Other Minds, and must be brought to sociality or allocentrism through development and learning. In its baldest form, this is the doctrine of initial primary process in terms of which even the first perceptions of the child are said to be little more than hallucinatory wish-fulfillments.

2. *Privacy.* That there is some inherently individualistic Self that develops, determined by the universal nature of man, and that it is beyond culture. In some deep sense, this Self is assumed to be ineffable, private. It is socialized, finally, by such processes as identification and internalization: the outer, public world becoming represented in the inner, private one.

3. *Unmediated conceptualism.* That the child's growing knowledge of the world is achieved principally by direct encounters with that world rather than mediated through vicarious encounters with it in interacting and negotiating with others. This is the doctrine of the child going it alone in mastering his knowledge of the world.

4. *Tripartism.* That cognition, affect, and action are represented by separate processes that, with time and socialization, come to interact with one another. Or the opposite view: that the three stem from a common process and that, with growth, they differentiate into autonomous systems. In either case, cognition is the late bloomer, the weak vessel, and is socially blind.

I do not want to argue that these four premises are "wrong," only that they are arbitrary, partial, and deeply rooted in the morality of our own culture. They are true under certain conditions, false under others, and their "universalization" reflects cultural bias. Their acceptance as universals, moreover, inhibits the development of a workable theory of the nature of social transaction and, indeed, even of the concept of Self. One could argue against the tenet of privacy, for example (inspired by anthropologists), that the distinction between "private self" and "public self" is a function of the culture's conventions about when one talks and negotiates the meanings of events and when one keeps silent, and of the ontological status given to that which is kept silent and that which is made public. Cultures and subcultures differ in this regard; so even do families.

❧

But let us return now to the main point: to the nature of transaction and the "executive processes" necessary to effect it, to those transactional selves hinted at in the title of this chapter. Consider in more detail now what the mastery of language entails with respect to these ideas.

Take *syntax* first. We need not pause long over it. The main point that needs making is that the possession of language gives us rules for generating well-formed utterances, whether they depend on the genome, upon experience, or upon some interaction of the two. Syntax provides a highly abstract system for accomplishing communicative functions that are crucial for regulating joint attention and joint action, for creating topics and commenting upon them in a fashion that segments "reality," for forefronting and imposing perspectives on events, for indicating our stance toward the world to which we refer and toward our interlocutors, for triggering presuppositions, and so on. We may not "know" all these things about our language in any explicit way (unless we happen to have that special form of consciousness which linguists develop), but what we do know from the earliest entry into language is that others can be counted upon to use the same rules of syntax for forming and for comprehending utterances as we use. It is so pervasive a system of calibration that we take it for granted. It entails not just the formulas of Grice, or of Sperber and Wilson, or of Putnam to which I referred, but the assurance that mind is being used by others as we use it. Syntax indeed entails a particular use of mind, and however much one may argue (as Joseph Greenberg in his way and Noam Chomsky in his have argued) that we cannot even conceive of alternative ways of using our minds, that language expresses our natural "organs of thought," it is still the case that the joint and mutual use of language gives us a huge step in the direction of understanding other minds. For it is not simply that we all *have* forms of mental organization that are akin, but that we *express* these forms constantly in our transactions with one another. We can count on constant transactional calibration in language, and we have ways of calling for repairs in one another's utterances to assure such calibration. And when we encounter those who do not share the means for this mutual calibration (as with foreigners), we regress, become suspicious, border on the paranoid, shout.

Language is also our principal means of *referring*. In doing so, it uses cues to the context in which utterances are being made and triggers presuppositions that situate the referent (matters discussed in Chapter 2). Indeed, reference plays upon the shared presuppositions and shared contexts of speakers. It is to the credit of Gareth Evans that he recognized the profound extent to which referring involves the mapping of speakers' subjective spheres on one another. He reminds us, for example, that even a failed effort to refer is not just a failure, but rather that it is an offer, an invitation to another to search possible contexts with us for a possible referent. In this sense, referring to something with the intent of directing another's attention to it requires even at its simplest some form of negotiation, some hermeneutic process. And it becomes the more so when the reference is not present or accessible to pointing or to some other ostensive maneuver. Achieving joint reference is achieving a kind of solidarity with somebody. The achievement by the child of such "intersubjective" reference comes so easily, so naturally, that it raises puzzling questions.

The evidence from early pointing (usually achieved before the first birthday) and from the infant's early following of another's line of regard suggests that there must be something preadapted and prelinguistic that aids us in achieving initial linguistic reference. I do not doubt the importance of such a biological assist. But this early assist is so paltry in comparison to the finished achievement of reference that it cannot be the whole of the story. The capacity of the average speaker to handle the subtleties of ellipsis, of anaphora—to know that, in the locution "Yesterday I saw *a* bird; *the* bird was singing," the shift from indefinite to definite article signals that the same bird is referred to in the second phrase as in the first—is too far removed from its prelinguistic beginnings to be accounted for by them. One has to conclude that the subtle and systematic basis upon which linguistic reference itself rests must reflect a natural organization of mind, one into which we *grow* through experience rather than one we achieve by learning.

If this is the case—and I find it difficult to resist—then human beings must come equipped with the means not only to calibrate the workings of their minds against one another, but to calibrate the worlds in which they live through the subtle means of reference. In effect, then, this is the means whereby we know Other Minds and their possible worlds.

The relation of words or expressions to other words or expressions constitutes, along with reference, the sphere of *meaning*. Because reference rarely achieves the abstract punctiliousness of a "singular, definite referring expression," is always subject to *polysemy,* and because there is no limit on the ways in which expressions can relate to one another, meaning is always underdetermined, ambiguous. To "make sense" in language, as David Olson argued persuasively some years ago, always requires an act of "disambiguation." Young children are not expert at such disambiguation, but procedures for effecting it are there from the earliest speech. They negotiate—even at two years of age—not only what is being referred to by an expression, but what other expressions the present one relates to. And children's early monologues, reported by Ruth Weir a generation ago and more recently by Katherine Nelson and her colleagues in the New York Language Acquisition Group, all point to a drive to explore and to overcome ambiguities in the meaning of utterances. The young child seems not only to negotiate sense in his exchanges with others but to carry the problems raised by such ambiguities back into the privacy of his own monologues. The realm of meaning, curiously, is not one in which we ever live with total comfort. Perhaps it is this discomfort that drives us finally to construct those larger-scale products of language—drama and science and the disciplines of understanding—where we can construct new forms in which to transact and negotiate this effort after meaning.

To create hypothetical entities and fictions, whether in science or in narrative, requires yet another power of language that, again, is early within reach of the language user. This is the capacity of language to create and stipulate realities of its own, its *constitutiveness*. We create realities by warning, by encouraging, by dubbing with titles, by naming, and by the manner in which words invite us to create "realities" in the world to correspond with them. Constitutiveness gives an externality and an apparent ontological status to the concepts words embody: for example, the law, gross national product, antimatter, the Renaissance. It is what makes us construct proscenia in our theater and still be tempted to stone the villain. At our most unguarded, we are all Naive Realists who believe not only that *we* know what is "out there," but also that it is out there for *others* as well. Carol Feldman calls it "ontic dumping," converting our mental processes into products and endowing them with a reality in some world. The private is rendered public. And thereby, once again, we locate ourselves in a world of shared reality. The constitutiveness of language, as more than one anthropologist has insisted, creates and transmits culture and locates our place in it—a matter to which I turn next.

Language, as we know, consists not only of a locution, of what is actually said, but of an illocutionary force—a conventional means of indicating what is intended by making that locution under those circumstances. These together constitute the speech acts of ordinary language, and they might be considered as much the business of the anthropologist as of the linguist. I will revisit the psychological implications of speech acts in a later chapter; here we need only take them for granted as a phenomenon. As a phenomenon, they imply that learning how to use language involves both learning the culture and learning how to express intentions in congruence with the culture. This brings us to the question of how we may conceive of "culture" and in what way it provides means not only for transacting with others but for conceiving of ourselves in such transactions.

❧

It would not be an exaggeration to say that in the last decade there has been a revolution in the definition of human culture. It takes the form of a move away from the strict structuralism that held that culture was a set of interconnected rules from which people derive particular behaviors to fit particular situations, to the idea of culture as implicit and only semiconnected knowledge of the world from which, through negotiation, people arrive at satisfactory ways of acting in given contexts. The anthropologist Clifford Geertz likens the process of acting in a culture to that of interpreting an ambiguous text. Let me quote a paragraph written by one of his students, Michelle Rosaldo:

> In anthropology, I would suggest, the key development . . . is a view of culture . . . wherein meaning is proclaimed a public fact—or better yet, where culture and meaning are described as processes of interpretive apprehension by individuals of symbolic models. These models are both

> "of" the world in which we live and "for" the organization of activities, responses, perceptions and experiences by the conscious self. For present purposes, what is important here is first of all the claim that meaning is a fact of public life, and secondly, that cultural patterns—social facts—provide the template for all human action, growth and understanding. Culture so construed is, furthermore, a matter less of artifacts and propositions, rules, schematic programs, or beliefs, than of associative chains and images that tell what can be reasonably linked up with what; we come to know it through collective stories that suggest the nature of coherence, probability and sense within the actor's world. Culture is, then, always richer than the traits recorded in the ethnographer's accounts because its truth resides not in explicit formulations of the rituals of daily life but in the daily practices of persons who in acting take for granted an account of who they are and how to understand their fellows' moves.

I have already discussed the linguistics, so to speak, by which this is accomplished. What of the "cultural" side of the picture? *How* we decide to enter into transaction with others linguistically and by what exchanges, how *much* we wish to do so (in contrast to remaining "detached" or "silent" or otherwise "private"), will shape our sense of what constitutes culturally acceptable transactions and our definition of our own scope and possibility in doing so—our "selfhood." As Rosaldo reminds us (using the Ilongot people as contrast) our Western concern with "individuals and with their inner hidden selves may well be features of *our* world of action and belief—itself to be explained and not assumed as the foundation of cross-cultural study." Indeed, the images and stories that we provide for guidance to speakers with respect to when they may speak and what they may say in what situations may indeed be a first constraint on the nature of selfhood. It may be one of the many reasons why anthropologists (in contrast to psychologists) have always been attentive not only to the content but to the form of the myths and stories they encounter among their "subjects."

For stories define the range of canonical characters, the settings in which they operate, the actions that are permissible and comprehensible. And thereby they provide, so to speak, a map of possible roles and of possible worlds in which action, thought, and self-definition are permissible (or desirable). As we enter more actively into the life of a culture around us, as Victor Turner remarks, we come increasingly to play parts defined by the "dramas" of that culture. Indeed, in time the young entrant into the culture comes to define his own intentions and even his own history in terms of the characteristic cultural dramas in which he plays a part—at first family dramas, but later the ones that shape the expanding circle of his activities outside the family.

It can never be the case that there is a "self" independent of one's cultural-historical existence. It is usually claimed, in classical philosophical texts at least, that Self rises out of our capacity to reflect upon our own acts, by the operation of "metacognition." But what is strikingly plain in the promising research on metacognition that has appeared in recent years—work by Ann Brown, by J. R. Hayes, by David Perkins, and others—is that metacognitive activity (self-monitoring and self-correction) is very unevenly distributed, varies according to cultural background, and, perhaps most important, can be taught successfully as a skill. Indeed, the available research on "linguistic repairs," self-corrections in utterances either to bring one's utterances into line with one's intent or to make them comprehensible to an interlocutor, suggests that an *Anlage* of metacognition is present as early as the eighteenth month of life. How much and in what form it develops will, it seems reasonable to suppose, depend upon the demands of the culture in which one lives—represented by particular others one encounters and by some notion of a "generalized other" that one forms (in the manner so brilliantly suggested by writers as various and as separated in time as St. Augustine in the *Confessions* and George Herbert Mead in *Mind, Self, and Society*).

It would seem a warranted conclusion, then, that our "smooth" and easy transactions and the regulatory self that executes them, starting as a biological readiness based on a primitive appreciation of other minds, is then reinforced and enriched by the calibrational powers that language bestows, is given a larger-scale map on which to operate by the culture in which transactions take place, and ends by being a reflection of the history of that culture as that history is contained in the culture's images, narratives, and tool kit.

In the light of the foregoing, we would do well to reexamine the tenets of the classical position on egocentrism with which we began:

Egocentric perspective. Michael Scaife and I discovered, as I mentioned in passing, that by the end of the first year of life, normal children habitually follow another's line of regard to see what the other is looking at, and when they can find no target out there, they turn back to the looker to check gaze direction again. At that age the children can perform none of the classic Piagetian tasks indicating that they have passed beyond egocentrism. This finding led me to take very seriously the proposals of both Katherine Nelson and Margaret Donaldson that when the child understands the event structure in which he is operating he is not that different from an adult. He simply does not have as grand a collection of scripts and scenarios and event schemas as adults do. The child's mastery of deictic shifters suggests, moreover, that egocentrism per se is not the problem. It is when the child fails to grasp the structure of events that he adopts an egocentric framework. The problem is not with competence but with performance. It is not that the child does not have the capacity to take another's perspective, but rather that he cannot do so without understanding the situation in which he is operating.

Privacy. The notion of the "private" Self free of cultural definition is part of the stance inherent in our Western conception of Self. The nature of the "untold" and the "untellable" and our attitudes toward them are deeply cultural in character. Private impulses are defined as such by the culture. Obviously, the divide between "private" and "public" meanings prescribed by a given culture makes a great difference in the way people in that culture view such meanings. In our culture, for example, a good deal of heavy emotional weather is made out of the distinction, and there is (at least among the educated) a push to get the private into the public domain—whether through confession or psychoanalysis. To revert to Rosaldo's Ilongot, the pressures are quite different for them, and so is the divide. How a culture defines privacy plays an enormous part in what people feel private *about* and when and how—as we have already seen in Amélie Rorty's account of personhood in Chapter 2.

Unmediated conceptualism. In the main, we do not construct a reality solely on the basis of private encounters with exemplars of natural states. Most of our approaches to the world are mediated through negotiation with others. It is this truth that gives such extraordinary force to Vygotsky's theory of the zone of proximal development, to which I shall turn in the next chapter. We know far too little about learning from vicarious experience, from interaction, from media, even from tutors.

Tripartism. I hope that all of the foregoing underlines the poverty that is bred by making too sharp a distinction between cognition, affect, and action, with cognition as the late-blooming stepsister. David Krech used to urge that people "perfink"—perceive, feel, and think at once. They also *act* within the constraints of what they "perfink." We *can* abstract each of these functions from the unified whole, but if we do so too rigidly we lose sight of the fact that it is one of the functions of a culture to keep them related and together in those images, stories, and the like by which our experience is given coherence and cultural relevance. The scripts and stories and "loose associative chains" that Rosaldo spoke of are templates for canonical ways of fusing the three into self-directing patterns—ways of being a Self in transaction. In Chapter 8, on the relation of thought and emotion, I shall take up this matter in more detail.

Finally, I want briefly to relate what I have said in this chapter to the discussions of narrative in the chapters of Part One. Insofar as we account for our own actions and for the human events that occur around us principally in terms of narrative, story, drama, it is conceivable that our sensitivity to narrative provides the major link between our own sense of self and our sense of others in the social world around us. The common coin may be provided by the forms of narrative that the culture offers us. Again, life could be said to imitate art.

5

The Inspiration of Vygotsky

There used to be a half-joking distinction made between paleo- and neo-Pavlovian psychology. That was in the late 1950s. Before that, we knew only about the former. Perhaps the latter had not yet been born. Or perhaps it was that what we were then hearing about the later Pavlov at second hand made him sound gaga. The *real* Pavlov was about conditioned reflexes—and what he dealt with was even called "classical conditioning" to distinguish it from such latecomers as instrumental and operant conditioning. The heart of the idea was that a conditioned stimulus "substituted" for the old unconditioned stimulus—a buzzer associated with food would now produce salivation just as the food had. I think it was Edward Tolman who first dubbed all such views of learning "switchboard theories."

As for neo-Pavlovian ideas, leaving aside the rumors of his gaga theories of personality that drifted to the West, they began to appear not so much on their own as in the form of a justification for other Russian work—particularly the work of Vygotsky and his devoted student, Luria. The phrase one heard (taken from Pavlov's later writings) was "the Second Signal System": the world as processed through language in contrast to the world of the senses. It was vague but interesting. We began to learn more about it when the Russians began coming in force to international congresses. I attended the one in Montreal in 1954. There was a big Russian delegation. Their papers characteristically started with a genuflection to Pavlov, followed abruptly by interesting accounts of studies of attention or problem solving that seemed to have little to do with the paleo-Pavlov I had read.

Then came the classical Russian reception at the end of the week of meetings, replete with the customary vodka and barrel of caviar. It was at that reception (and at an informal party afterwards at Wilder Penfield's) that I first encountered talk of Vygotsky's influence, of his work on the role of language in development, of the "Zone of Proximal Development," and of the role of the Second Signal System in all this. The Second Signal System, the world encoded in language, stood for nature transformed by history and culture. In fact, Pavlov had done little with the idea. Vygotsky had, and so too had his coterie of brilliant students. Vygotsky's work, I learned that evening, was widely circulated in Russia, though it was officially banned. The Second Signal System was the perfect Marxist vehicle for vaulting beyond old Pavlov while still maintaining a posture of high respect for him as an ikon. It was to be the vehicle by which Vygotsky would be put back in circulation after having disgraced himself by delving too deeply into cultural differences in intelligence in earlier studies of farmers in Uzbeki and Khirghistan collectives.

The major premise in Vygotsky's formulation (Marxist in his opinion, though advanced for its times and certainly regarded with suspicion by the official ideologists then in power) was the view that man was subject to the dialectical play between nature and history, between his qualities as a creature of biology and as a product of human culture. It risked being tagged as "bourgeois idealism," for mental activity was given a dangerously dominant place in the system. Yet, as Raymond Bauer has pointed out in his book on those times, it was a necessary corrective to the passive environmental determinism of the early Pavlov. That view was fit only for victims of an old environment that could be blamed for the old troubles. Now the Soviet Union was building a new environment, one shaped by Plans. That required mind, mind that could rise above the circumstances the State had inherited from the past.

Vygotsky's *Thought and Language* was first published in Russian in 1934, shortly after his death of tuberculosis at the age of thirty-eight. The authorities found it too mental, too idealist. Or perhaps it fell victim to the paranoia and anti-Semitism of the Stalinist purges. It was suppressed in 1936. As Luria and Leontiev said of the book two decades later, "The first and most important task of that time [the late 1920s and 1930s when the 'battle for consciousness' raged] consisted of freeing oneself on the one hand from vulgar behaviorism and, on the other, from the subjective approach to mental phenomena as exclusively inner subjective conditions that can only be investigated introspectively." It was not for twenty years that the book could appear openly in Russian. It was republished in 1956, the same year in which historians of science place the "birth" of the Cognitive Revolution. Something was altering the intellectual atmosphere, something that Vygotsky had helped foment.

Vygotsky's book finally appeared in English in 1962. I was asked to write an introduction to it. By then I had learned enough about Vygotsky from Alexander Romanovich Luria, with whom I had become close friends, that I welcomed this added goad to close study. I read the translation-in-progress with meticulous care, and with growing astonishment. For Vygotsky was plainly a genius. Yet it was an elusive form of genius. In contrast to, say, Piaget, there was nothing massive or glacial about the flow of his thought or about its development. Rather, it was like the later Wittgenstein: at times aphoristic, often sketchy, vivid in its illuminations.

To begin with, I liked his instrumentalism, his way of interpreting thought and speech as instruments for the planning and carrying out of action. Or as he put it in an early essay, "Children solve practical tasks with the help of their speech, as well as with their eyes and hands. This unity of perception, speech and action, which ultimately produces internalization of the visual field, constitutes the central subject matter for any analysis of the origin of uniquely human forms of behavior" (*Mind in Society,* p. 26). Language is (in Vygotsky's sense as in Dewey's) a way of sorting out one's thoughts about things. Thought is a mode of organizing perception and action. But all of them, each in their way, also reflects the tools and aids available in the culture for use in carrying out action. Take the epigraph from Francis Bacon with which Vygotsky begins *Thought and Language*, "Nec manus, nisi intellectus, sibi permissus, multam valent; instrumentis et auxilibus res perficitur." But what a curious epigraph: neither the hand nor the mind alone, left to itself, would amount to much. And what are these prosthetic devices that perfect them (if I may be permitted a modern gloss on "instrumentis et auxilibus")?

Well, for one thing, society provides a tool kit of concepts and ideas and theories that permit one to get to higher ground mentally. "The new higher concepts in turn transform the meaning of the lower. The adolescent who has mastered algebraic concepts has gained a vantage point from which he sees arithmetic concepts in a broader perspective" (*Thought and Language*, p. 115). They provide a means for turning around upon one's thoughts, for seeing them in a new light. This is, of course, mind reflecting on itself. Not surprising, given the plodding, *lumpen* Marxist criticism and interpretation of those days, that Vygotsky was banned for twenty years. Consciousness plays an enormous role, consciousness armed with concepts and the language for forming and transforming them.

About consciousness he says: "Consciousness and control appear only at a late stage in the development of a function, after it has been used and practiced unconsciously and spontaneously. In order to subject a function to intellectual control, we must first possess it" (ibid., p. 90). This suggests that prior to the development of self-directed, conscious control, action is, so to speak, a more direct or less mediated response to the world. Consciousness or *reflection* is a way of keeping mind from (if the mixed metaphor will be permitted) shooting from the hip. That much is familiar enough as a form of conscious inhibition. But what of the instruments by means of which mind now grapples itself to "higher ground"?

This is the heart of the matter, the point at which Vygotsky brings to bear his fresh ideas about the now famous Zone of Proximal Development (the ZPD hereafter). It is an account of how the more competent assist the young and the less competent to reach that higher ground, ground from which to reflect more abstractly about the nature of things. To use his words, the ZPD is the distance between the actual developmental level as determined by independent problem solving and the level of potential development as determined through problem solving under adult guidance or in collaboration with more capable peers" (*Mind in Society*, p. 86). "Human learning," he says, "presupposes a specific social nature and a process by which children grow into the intellectual life of those around them" (ibid., p. 88). And then, "Thus the notion of a zone of proximal development enables us to propound a new formula, namely that the only 'good learning' is that which is in advance of development" (ibid., p. 89).

There seems, however, to be a contradiction. On the one hand, consciousness and control can come only *after* the child has already got a function well and spontaneously mastered. So how could this "good learning" be achieved in advance of spontaneous development since, as it were, the child's unmasterly reaction to a task would be bound initially to be unconscious and unreflective? How can the competent adult "lend" consciousness to a child who does not "have" it on his own? What is it that makes possible this implanting of vicarious consciousness in the child by his adult tutor? It is as if there were a kind of scaffolding erected for the learner by the tutor. But how?

Nowhere in Vygotsky's writings is there any concrete spelling out of what he means by such scaffolding. But I think I can reconstruct his intentions from two sources, one of them philosophical-historical and in Vygotsky's own hand, so to speak, the other from research on such "scaffolding" that I undertook myself, better to grasp what this intriguing concept might mean.

Philosophically, there is a hidden agenda in Vygotsky's account, and it needs to be made explicit. He believed that "modernization" of the peasant through collectivization and mechanization could be described in the same way as one described the growth of the child from prescientific to scientific thinking. In both, there was a creative fusing of collective action and consciousness—a fuzzy notion that will, I think, come clear shortly. For him that "fusing" was primary to the human division of labor. He believed that the transmission of mind across history is effected by successive mental sharings that assure a passing on of ideas from the more able or advanced to the less so. And the medium in which the transmission occurs is language and its products: literacy, science, technology, literature. Recall that when Vygotsky went to Uzbekistan and Khirgizia to do his studies on changing peasant mentality, literacy was a passionate topic. Writing and reading were not only practically desirable. They were to "modernize" the mind. And there was even a school of Russian symbolist painters (vividly described and well illustrated in Robert Hughes's book on the modernist tradition) that was to convert consciousness by new techniques of graphic design. The general idea was widespread among literary intellectuals and linguists of the day—the Formalist poets and men like Bakhtin and Jakobson and Troubetskoy, whom Vygotsky either knew personally or admired. He had, after all, written a book on the psychology of art that focused principally on literature. Language, whether in art or in science, reflected our lives in history. Yet at the same time it could propel us beyond history.

But that is all very grand and, as Roman Jakobson once remarked to me, more Russian than socialist, more literary than linguistic, more philosophical than psychological. Indeed, it comes out of the same mold as Jakobson's idea as a young man to create consciousness through literary devices that made the world strange again—a cornerstone of his poetics discussed in an earlier chapter. Yet, I think this ingenious intuition can be given a psychological rendering. So let me turn to the empirical research that can help us to it.

First, studies of tutoring and what makes it effective. Until very recently, there were very few studies of tutoring—for the very reason I mentioned in the preceding chapter: the child was studied as a lone agent mastering the world on his own. Some years ago, David Wood, Gail Ross, and I decided to have a close look at what actually happens in a tutoring pair when one, in possession of knowledge, attempts to pass it on to another who does not possess it. The task we chose (because it allowed us to observe what the child was doing) was teaching children to build a pyramid out of a set of interlocking wooden blocks. The tutor, Dr. Ross, was not only knowledgeable about children but genuinely interested in what they were doing and how they could be helped. That part mattered, but we can pass it by here and return to it in a later chapter on the relation of thought and emotion. All we need note here is that she turned the task into play and caught it in a narrative that gave it continuity.

What emerged was, I suppose, obvious enough. She was indeed "consciousness for two" for the three- and five-year-olds she tutored, and in many ways. To begin with, it was she who controlled the focus of attention. It was she who, by slow and often dramatized presentation, demonstrated the task to be possible. She was the one with a monopoly on foresight. She kept the segments of the task on which the child worked to a size and complexity appropriate to the child's powers. She set things up in such a way that the child could *recognize* a solution and perform it later even though the child could neither do it on his own nor follow the solution when it was simply *told* to him. In this respect, she made capital out of the "zone" that exists between what people can recognize or comprehend when present before them, and what they can generate on their own—and that is the Zone of Proximal Development, or the ZPD. In general, what the tutor *did* was what the child could *not* do. For the rest, she made things such that the child could do *with* her what he plainly could not do *without* her. And as the tutoring proceeded, the child took over from her parts of the task that he was not able to do at first but, with mastery, became consciously able to do under his own control. And she gladly handed those over. (Interestingly, when the observations were repeated years later using young children as tutors for younger children, they were not as different as expected, save in one crucial respect: the young tutors would not hand over parts of the task as the younger child achieved mastery.)

Obviously, not everybody is a genius in serving as a "vicarious consciousness" for others. But David Wood's later work on tutoring surely indicates that tutoring is a skill that can be learned. One final, rather rueful finding from another study leads me to think that there may even be little microcultures, sometimes as small as families or human pairs, that aid or destroy the "skill" involved. The English psychologist Barbara Tizard reports a study in which she sought to correlate the "interestingness" of children's questions with the "goodness" of the replies that parents give to them. The rueful finding is this. The more likely parents are to give good answers, the more likely are children to ask interesting questions. But, on the other hand, given the nature of correlations, the finding can be stated in the reverse direction: the more likely children are to ask interesting questions, the more likely parents are to give good answers. So while there are specific things to be said about the "loan of consciousness" from the more able to the less, what is involved is surely not a simple act of will but a negotiable transaction.

Vygotsky himself remarks that the acquisition of language provides the paradigm case for what he is talking about, for it is in the nature of things that the aspirant speaker must "borrow" the knowledge and consciousness of the tutor to enter a language. And there are two observations that give vivid specificity to his point. The first comes from studies of language acquisition I did at Oxford. Those studies reveal one durable regularity in mother-child interaction during language acquisition. It is the mother who establishes little "formats" or rituals in which language is used: "book reading" routines with picture books, request patterns, little games, and so on. She plays her part in them with striking regularity. In book reading, for example, she phases her questions in a regular sequence: (1) Vocative, (2) Query, (3) Label, (4) Confirmation. Or, (1) Oh look, Richard! (2) What's that? (3) It's a fishy. (4) That's right. This sequence provides a scaffold for "teaching" reference. At the start, the infant may understand little. His response to the query may then develop and take the form of a babble. And once that occurs, the mother will thereafter insist on *some* response in that slot of the scaffold. Once the child alters his responding babble to a word-length vocalization, she will again raise the ante and not accept a babble, but only the shorter version. Eventually, when the name of a referent is mastered, she will shift to a game in which the given and the new are to be separated. Whereas before, "What's that?" was spoken with a rising terminal stress, now it receives a falling terminal stress, as if to indicate that she knows that the child knows the answer. To which he typically responds with a new show of coyness. And shortly after, she raises the ante again: "What's the fishy doing?" with rising terminal stress anew as she takes him into the ZPD again, this time to master predication. She remains forever on the growing edge of the child's competence.

Which led Roger Brown to ask how it could be that in transmitting a language mothers invariably talk at just the level of complexity that the child already can understand. What can the child learn from *that*? Brown's answer is that the child is being given an opportunity to master meanings in new contexts, better to understand what language is about and what it can do. Vygotsky would have said, had he known of this regularity, that the mother was providing an opportunity for the child to achieve his own consciousness, that up to that point he was using hers as a crutch to get beyond infant speech.

In my own work, I concluded that any innate Language Acquisition Device, LAD, that helps members of our species to penetrate language could not possibly succeed but for the presence of a Language Acquisition Support System, LASS, provided by the social world, that is matched to LAD in some regular way. It is LASS that helps the child navigate across the Zone of Proximal Development to full and conscious control of language use.

While I think there are enormous differences between the way language is acquired and the ways other forms of knowledge and skill are

rules. We know from previous chapters that context is crucial to the decoding of an utterance—as with those deictic shifters like *here* and *there*. We know too that, given the nature of speech acts, the locution embodied in an utterance (though it must be parsed to be comprehended) is not all that the live listener is digging out of a sentence.

Yet, although my friend's effort is now considered a failure (especially by him), it must be considered a brilliant one, indeed a fruitful one. For *his* was not the failure. The failure was in the model of language whose psychological reality he chose to test. Its claims were exaggerated, not the nature of George Miller's enterprise (for I had just as well name its author). What in fact he was doing was trying to establish the validity of linguistic descriptions in the domain of psychology. Or to put it more bluntly (and controversially), he was making a claim for the utility of "psycholinguistics" as an enterprise, arguing that you cannot have a psychology that proposes to "explain" language that is at the same time unmindful of linguistic distinctions, or perhaps, a linguistics that is unmindful of how speakers and listeners, readers and writers, handle language. (The latter claim is considerably more debatable, for there is no a priori reason to suppose that a formal description of language must be known or knowable to speakers to be useful as a scientific account—as Carol Feldman and Stephen Toulmin have argued in their paper "Logic and the Theory of Mind.") The former claim—that psychology *can* provide an account of language without embracing linguistic knowledge—had been altogether too widespread and deserved to be attacked. Else we would be forever burdened with St. Augustine's "imitation-cum-association" account of how the child acquires language, or with B. F. Skinner's operant conditioning explanation.

If today we were to make the case for the "psychological reality" of linguistic structures (and it still needs making, despite the huge and luxuriant growth of psycholinguistics in the last three decades), it would not be so different in spirit from that early attempt to establish the reality of grammar. The difference would be in the *range* of what we would want to take into account in the nature of language as a phenomenon. The effort would certainly *not* be limited to demonstrating the "psychological" reality of the rules of syntax or phonology or semantics, though it would be the height of folly to exclude these from the final account. For it is in the nature of language, as I have already noted briefly, that it is governed by the principle of "duality of functioning" or, more simply, by top-down rules. To be more specific, the distinctive features of the sound system that constitute a language are determined by the limited set of phonemes employed in constructing the next unit up, morphemes. And morphology is determined by the uses to which morphemes are put in forming lexemes or words. Words, in their turn, are formally describable by the functions they perform in sentences. Sentences, in turn, achieve their significance from the discourse in which they are embedded. Discourse is governed by the communicative intentions of speakers. The communicative intentions of speakers, of course, are governed by the transactional requirements of the culture. And along the way, there are further determinants of form that operate in this same dualistic way. I commented in an earlier chapter, for example, on the importance of *genre* in determining how discourse may be interpreted. This top-down interdependence, moreover, applies even to such larger-scale linguistic products as folktales, as we have already seen in considering Vladimir Propp's analysis of "characters" as functions of the plot.

❧

Indeed, what I want to do in this chapter is to consider the "psychological reality" of some of the linguistic distinctions that have been passed in review in previous chapters. I have, to be sure, been trying to make the case for their reality *en passant,* but it would be well to pause here for a closer accounting. And given the "duality" principle, the top-downness of language, I must begin by taking a fresh look at the different criteria by which language can be assessed as a phenomenon.

The usual way to begin such an inquiry is by reference to three traditional aspects of language. The first, the syntactic, rests on the criterion of well-formedness, or conformity to the grammatical rules that are hypothesized to govern the language. It does not matter greatly for purposes of assessing well-formedness whether the grammar the scientist uses is psychologically real: the grammars prescribing well-formedness can be as abstract and "unlifelike" as necessary, depending upon what one is trying to do. A "good grammar" (a good generative grammar, that is) is one that will generate all possible permissible sentences of a language and none that is impermissible.

The second aspect that provides criteria for assessing language phenomena is meaning. Here the task becomes more difficult, because it requires a theory about sense and about reference, and there is nothing that corresponds in this domain to the precise descriptions by which well-formedness is judged. You can, of course, judge once for all the well-formedness of the expression "Colorless green ideas sleep furiously," but you can say nothing of equal definitiveness about the meaning of the expression. What you *can* do is to specify various procedures for assigning meaning to the utterance. But then you will be caught between contending views—verificationist theories of meaning, correspondence theories, congruence theories, all of which are partial. Or you can have recourse to a dictionary and look up all the individual words in the utterance—like C. K. Ogden's philosopher who, not finding an encyclopedia entry for "Chinese metaphysics," looked up "China" and "metaphysics." Or, so to speak, you can let your mind travel by metaphoric trope, in which case you will, indeed, end up assigning some interesting meanings. For example, for "Powerless green ideas sleep furiously," you can read "Rejected, once promising theories lie angrily on the conscience." Or, "Noam Chomsky in his salad days." Or, as we did in Chapter 2, you can inquire whether an expression triggers many alternative meanings and leads to reflection thereby. There are many interesting ways of pursuing meaning, a good many of them vividly illustrated in a stout book by George Miller and Philip Johnson-Laird, *Language and Perception*, and in John Lyons's two-volume *Semantics*. But in the end there remain some hopeless puzzles: like what size of unit should you assign a meaning *to*, a word, a sentence, a speech act, a discourse, a Wittgensteinian language game?

Which leads directly to the third criterion: the pragmatic one. It is presumed to deal with *use*. Traditionally (in Charles Morris's *Signs, Language and Behavior*, where the distinctions among syntax, semantics, and pragmatics were frozen into a linguistic trinity), pragmatics was supposed to deal with how people used their language, in contrast to how the language was structured syntactically and what it meant semantically. This, presumably, included a motley range of things such as rhetoric, propaganda, perhaps poetics. It was, of course, naive (even for the 1940s, when Morris published his book) to assume that meaning was independent of the uses to which a speaker put his language (as in modern speech acts) or of the psychic interpretant the listener brought to bear upon the message to which he was assigning a meaning. For Morris, pragmatics was something "added on" to semantics and syntax, something that yet somehow did not change the other two dominions.

From the very start, I think, it has been clear that looking at language separately "in the light" of well-formedness, of meaning, and of use was more a pedagogical convenience than a genuine intellectual undertaking. And the reasons why this is so may shed some light on our quest for the "psychological reality" of language and language-mediated phenomena.

Take first the issue of the autonomy of syntax. There are, as we know, those who argue that the syntactical rules of language derive from initial semantic requirements. One of them, Charles Fillmore, has argued that humans first understood the arguments of action, out of which a case grammar was derived for representing not only ACTION but also its arguments, AGENT, OBJECT, RECIPIENT, INSTRUMENT, LOCATION, and so on. Cases eventually are abstracted into grammatical classes of a more abstract nature and are assigned privileges of occurrence in sentences, and so on. This is a difficult case to sustain logically (for it fails to account for certain evident grammatical distinctions), and impossible to prove historically. Yet, it is attractive as an account of the *acquisition* of language in the young child, and it has strongly influenced Roger Brown's landmark description.

Another view (originated by the Prague School) argues that grammar derives not so much from our abstract knowledge of action and its arguments, but from discourse. Subject and predicate, for example, are derived from topic and comment, topic being what is given and shared in discourse between speakers, comment what is being added as new. Some, like Ulric Neisser, have even gone so far as to argue that the given-new, the marked-unmarked distinction that is universal to language may derive from the figure-ground phenomenon in perception, the given being ground, figure constituting the new. Again, it scarcely serves the purpose of intellectual inquiry to reject out of hand the notion that syntax (so much the instrument of meaning and discourse) is autonomous from pragmatics either in its origins or in its function.

Just as syntax is dependent on semantics and pragmatics, so too semantics itself is dependent on the use to which an utterance is being put. Indeed, you *can* "look up" words, if not sentences, in dictionaries and find out what they mean. Or decompose meanings into their components—like, *murder* equals *cause to die* and *bachelor* is constituted of *unmarried* and *male*. But as H. P. Grice long ago pointed out, there are two kinds of meaning—timeless meaning and occasion meaning, the meaning of the locution per se and the meaning intended in the situation in which the locution was uttered. Dictionaries and decomposition will get you the former but not the latter. What *is* the meaning of a locution per se? Philosophers and linguists tend to treat the utterance as a proposition and not as a speech act driven by a specialized communicative intention. But isn't the result just another kind of occasion meaning?

Take the limiting case: whether or not to speak on a given occasion. In most instances of dialogue, silence is interpretable, has a meaning. So too in what one chooses to include and what to leave out of an utterance. The French linguist Oswald Ducrot has developed the intuitive claim, in his book *Dire et ne pas dire*, that speaking presupposes its contrast, the maintenance of silence. The contrast between the two, by his claim, is crucial for the deployment of presupposition in ordinary speech. What one does *not* utter is presupposed or given; what one does utter is new. On this view, spoken speech is used as a vehicle for establishing or maintaining an explicit attention to matters that cannot be taken for granted. In simple declarative speech acts, one does *not* indicate by overt speech that which one can take for granted as an element of knowledge or experience in the interlocutor's mind. I do not say "This room has walls" to my partner in conversation unless the matter is in question. Or, as Peter Wason noted twenty years ago, one uses a negative declaration "naturally" only under conditions of plausible denial, and resists saying things like "This table is not made of wax" unless there is some prior reason to take it for granted that some or many tables *are* made of wax. The use of negation presupposes a context that merits plausible denial. Even at this simplest level, utterances are governed by the requirements of discourse and dialogue rather than by some fixed and univocal semantic mapping of an expression onto some real-world or possible-world knowledge.

❧

The issue of speech acts and implicatures requires special attention in any such discussion as this one. For, in a sense, they represent most strikingly the fusion of the three frames of reference in terms of which language can be understood: the syntactic, the semantic, and the pragmatic. A speech act, of course, is a conventionalized means of embodying an intention in a message. John Searle first proposed that there are at least three conditions that must be met when we perform such typical speech acts as indicating, requesting, promising, warning, and so on: *preparatory, essential,* and *sincerity* conditions, to which I would add an *affiliative* condition as a fourth. Preparatory conditions require a tuning of the hearer's attention to the issue at hand: that this is a request or a warning or a promise. Essential conditions define the logic of the act: you do not request something when you already possess it, nor warn against nonexistent dangers. Sincerity conditions specify that the intent of the speech act be genuine: you do not request something you do not want. An affiliative condition specifies that the utterance take account of the relation that exists between speaker and hearer. That old chestnut of pragmatics, "Would you be so kind as to pass the salt," provides an example. It is not a request for knowledge about the hearer's limits of compassion or kindness. Rather, it is a request for the salt that recognizes the voluntary or nonobligatory status of the hearer with respect to the speaker.

If speech acts are such a universal feature of language (or language use), it seems reasonable to suppose that the development of syntax, of semantics, and even of the lexicon would reflect the requirement of indicating intentions in speech. Obviously, there are many paralinguistic or expressive devices for aiding in this—intonation, prosody, and so on. But what of more formally linguistic devices? Carol Feldman and Charles Fillmore, working independently, are among those who have suggested that language is rich in both lexical elements and syntactic rules that have as virtually their sole object to make the speaker's perspective and stance clearer. Feldman offers as her example of such devices the phenomenon of "stance marking" by the use of such words as *even, only,* and *just.* It is virtually their only function in language. Take the set composed of variants on:

> John will marry Elsie.
> Even John will marry Elsie.
> John will even marry Elsie.
> John will marry even Elsie.

Note that each variant also imposes stress on the word that carries the burden of uncertainty—*John, marry,* and *Elsie* in the three variants.

Fillmore, for his part, raises the question of whether grammar is principally a device that permits speakers to set forth their "perspective on a scene." It is a more elaborated version of the "stance marking" of Feldman, and he makes the more ambitious claim that one of the major functions of grammar in general (rather than a subset of stance operators) is to accomplish this setting of perspective. As illustration, he notes the function of passive and active sentences in signaling the attentional perspective of the speaker, as in:

The Ming vase was overturned by the cat.
The cat overturned the Ming vase.

Again, stress follows the attentional focus in the head word of each utterance.

Indeed, Fillmore's example brings us full circle round, for it was precisely such optional transformations in language as passivization that occupied George Miller in that early quest for the reality of grammar. The other transformations were query and negation. The interrogative transformation is as transparent a syntactic indicator of speech-act intent as there is. And we have already seen from Wason's research how linked to the requirements of "plausible denial" in discourse is negation. The historical irony is that it was Wason's study, finally, that showed that negative sentences were sometimes more quickly processed and comprehended than untransformed kernel sentences—when conditions of plausible denial were present.

One final word about implicatures will link us to the earlier discussion of them in Chapter 2. Recall that they involve violating the conditions on speech acts (or the maxims of sincerity, relevance, brevity, and so on) in order to mean more than you say. In a sense, as I commented earlier, they bring into being a new class of linguistic devices for "carrying" the subtleties of discourse: irony, understatement, indirection, and tropes yet to be labeled. Speech acts and the maxims of conversation, in this version of the matter, not only use the devices already *in* the language for indicating stance and intent by conventional means, but they may in fact be the generators for producing new means.

That much said, we can return to the main argument—the psychological reality of language and the products that language creates. I have tried to show that it is self-defeating to establish the psychological reality or relevance of syntactical, semantic, and pragmatic distinctions, each on their own and in isolation from the others. Whatever use Morris's distinction may have in linguistics proper (the formal science of language with no regard to who is using it or how), it certainly has minimum utility for the psychologist of language. Everything is use. And whatever is used is syntactically organized accordingly and has some meaning that can be assigned to it by some speaker in some circumstance. Indeed, even so classically pragmatic a subject as "presupposition," examined carefully (as it has been recently in Gerald Gazdar's painstaking book on pragmatics), turns out to have as much connection to syntax and semantics as to "pragmatics." Presuppositions, as already remarked in an earlier chapter, are triggered by "devices" that are principally syntactic or lexical in nature and cannot be understood as a feature of language without those devices.

The only way to proceed, then, is to plunge directly into that feature of language whose psychological substrate one wishes to investigate and to discover through what psychological processes it is realized. Then we may ask how those processes are orchestrated in a fashion to make language possible—"real" language as used. That is to say, what makes a sentence "real" is the specification of the mental processes that produce it or permit its comprehension. It does not suffice, in carrying out this task, to invoke vague and general psychological processes like association or imitation. The processes must be shown to be adequate to deal with the linguistic structure of sentences (from NP-VP dominated by an S node, to clefting, ellipsis, or whatever). If it can also be shown that these processes then generate nonlinguistic side-effects, so much the more interesting. But it does nothing for the claim of the "psychological reality" of grammar to show that clicks sounded during the speaking of a sentence are heard not where they occurred (in the middle of a phrase), but displaced toward a phrase boundary. Would one claim the "psychological reality" of musical bar notation by demonstrating that clicks drift toward the edges of musical phrases?

More to the point, it is of little use to provide an account of the psychological processes underlying sentence grammar if, in doing so, one closes off the possibility of discovering how the sentence can serve as a speech act, or loses sight of its perspective-setting function at the semantic or pragmatic level.

The psychological reality of any linguistic description inheres not in our ability to account psychologically for particular properties specified by that description but in our ability to account, rather, for how language in all its linguistic complexity is used in fulfilling its myriad functions.

❧

Let me turn now to a second meaning of "reality." Most of what we deal with in the social world, I have urged repeatedly, could not exist but for a symbolic system that brings that world into existence: national or local loyalty, money, memberships, promises, political parties. The same can be said as well, though in somewhat different form, for the world of "nature," for our experience of nature is shaped by conceptions of it formed in discourse with others. The brunt of my argument in the opening chapters was that the "reality" of most of us is constituted roughly into two spheres: that of nature and that of human affairs, the former more likely to be structured in the paradigmatic mode of logic and science, the latter in the mode of story and narrative. The latter is centered around the drama of human intentions and their vicissitudes; the first around the equally compelling, equally natural idea of causation. The subjective reality that constitutes an individual's sense of his world is roughly divided into a natural and a human one.

Obviously, there are confusions and overlaps. Animism is one such: attributing intention to objects in the "natural" world that would, ordinarily, be viewed as causally determined. And radical behaviorism is another: attributing cause and denying the role of intention in the realm of human events. But it is usually the case (at least in Western culture) that people agree about which is which, and when they do not agree, the consequence is polemical—in battles about human descent where the *story* of creation is pitted against the *theory* of evolution. In any case, the confusions do not carry over into the practical sphere of action. For in practice, we manipulate or operate physically upon *that* which is in the domain of cause and effect; but we interact or try to communicate with *those* who seem governed by intentions. Or as the Navy adage had it, "salute it if it moves, otherwise paint it."

What can we say psychologically about such "psychological realities"? Again, I would argue that the problem is one of explaining the psychological processes that constitute them—in psychology, in anthropology, in everyday observation. Can such "standard" psychological processes as perception, inference, memory, thought account for the constructed realities? The question is not whether *two* sets of processes produce *two* different worlds, but how *any* processes could produce the world constructions we find.

❧

Begin with processes of inference, with two illustrative experiments that help make the matter clearer. The first is from a study by Henri Zukier and Albert Pepitone. It follows the classic studies of Daniel Kahnemann and Amos Tversky on the way in which people use probabilistic knowledge about past events in guiding their reaction to a present situation. You begin by reading a description of somebody:

> Steve is very shy and withdrawn, invariably helpful, but with little interest in people, or in the world of reality. A meek and tidy soul, he has a need for order and structure, and a passion for detail.

You present it to your subject as one of many drawn at random from a set of sketches of which seventy are salesmen and thirty librarians. Which is Steve, a salesman or a librarian? By base-rate reasoning, taking into account only the probabilities, your subject should say he is a salesman. That is the ultimate paradigmatic approach: to operate by the Bayes theorem that prescribes "riding with the probabilities." But give subjects a reason for embedding their judgment in a story, in a world of narrative, and they will ignore Bayesian probabilities.

Zukier and Pepitone show how one disposes subjects in one direction or the other by manipulating the amount of evocative context one provides them. They used two instructed orientations as provocations to the subjects to go in one of two directions: a " 'scientific' orientation . . . concerned with general propositions" that related individual performance to population norms, and a " 'clinical' orientation . . . concerned with understanding the individual case," by "constructing a coherent narrative, or 'case-history' of the person." Those exposed to the scientific mode judge in conformity with Bayesian probability. The others, disposed to construct clinical narratives, virtually ignore the Bayesian rule.

For reasons growing out of the rationalism of psychology, subjects who follow the logic of drama (that is, who act like clinicians or storytellers) are characterized in the literature on inference as "committing the base-rate fallacy." But Zukier and Pepitone object. For them, "the base-rate fallacy" is not just "an inappropriate application of normative criteria." It is the outcome of a different strategy, one that takes account of the context in which behavior occurs rather than focusing only on general tendencies, on behavior in a vacuum. To put it more directly, one group is constructing a reality of characters involved in particular actions in particular settings, a reality in which "base-rate information" is wholly irrelevant or, if relevant, chiefly so in guiding one in the construction of a "reasonable" narrative. Fallacy? Imagine a medical diagnostician using only the probabilities contained in his case files to decide whether a patient with a severe pain in his abdomen should be subjected to appendectomy. Would he be able to face the hospital tissue committee with the plea that he was operating according to Bayes? What is clear is that the "outcomes" achieved in inference when one uses Bayesian estimates are not "reality" in contrast to an "illusion" produced by operating clinically. Subjects who go the clinical route are operating "realistically" too, but in another reality. They are like those literary colleagues I mentioned in Chapter 1 who operate from the bottom up to construct a "reality" of this poem or that novel.

The second experiment to which I want to allude is one of my own, one that I did to correct an oversight in a previous study done nearly a quarter of a century before. The details are elaborate, and the reader can be spared. The experiment is, again, on one of those "classical" phenomena in human cognition, "concept attainment." Yet, while it is technical, it is at the heart of a great deal of everyday human activity. Concept attainment is the process through which, having encountered a great many particular instances, we decide that some subset of them form a category or class that is distinctive. And so, for example, we discover by test that only those mushrooms that are flatheaded, short, and tan can be eaten without ill effect, and we create the category of "edible mushrooms." Or we formulate a statute for Freedonia that only those over twenty-one who are propertyholders in the town and have been in residence for over a year are "eligible candidates for the town council." There are various kinds of categories or "concepts," formed by different rules of grouping and different ways of applying criteria for inclusion and exclusion. But while many of these technical considerations motivated the original experiments reported in *A Study of Thinking*, they were not what led me to undertake the reconstructive study.

It came into being in the following way. In doing experiments of this kind, one typically presents the subjects with a set of cards on each of which is exhibited a set of "attributes": each card will contain, say, one of two or three possible figures; each figure will be one of two or three different colors; whatever the figure and its color, it will be either large or small, and so on. The experiment is run as a guessing game. You tell your subject that you have in mind a particular kind of cards in the set that are "right" and others that are not, and that his job is to find out as quickly as possible which is which—whether, say, all the red ones are right, or the tall green ones, or the blue squares, or what. He is shown one at a time, asked to guess whether it is "right" or "wrong" and then told whether he was correct. Human beings are not spectacular performers (even a little computer can be rigged to do better than most of us), but they are reasonably good in eliminating irrelevant attributes and getting to what in fact defines "rightness" (that is, class inclusion) by some quite ingenious strategies. The phenomena one can observe in such a tiny experiment are sufficiently interesting to have bred a lively cottage research industry in concept attainment.

It so happened that in those original experiments there were included one set of cards whose attributes were a lot livelier and more "thematic" than the ones containing figures and colors and sizes. Each of these cards was a variant of something more "narratable," we would say now. Each contained a child and an adult. Either could be a male or a female. The adult or the child was either in night dress or in street clothes. The child was either happily holding his hands out (as if to receive something) or dejectedly holding hands behind his back; and the adult (as if to match) was either proffering an object or had hands clasped behind. Each card was a natural little scene for drama.

In the earlier study, we had found that subjects were slower in attaining the correct concept with these cards than they were with nonthematic cards matched for number of attributes. Faced with the "narrative" cards, they seemed to hang on to their hypotheses longer in the face of negative information, required more redundant input, and, on the whole, looked rather "dumber" logically than when having to deal with bare-boned attributes. And they were, of course, much more prone to bizarre hypotheses about what was right: for example, scenes depicting possible birthdays, rule transgressions, unhappy children, and the like. We duly reported their error-proneness in print but made nothing more of it.

When I redid the experiment recently (with Allison McCluer), keeping a verbatim record of what our subjects had to say in the proceedings, there were some surprises. Our subjects (not all, but some significant portion of them) were plainly involved in forming "dramatic hypotheses" and were not using the information contained in the attributes in any direct way to test whether they were relevant or not. A typical subject, for example, thought the positive or "right" cards all depicted a "happy relationship between a parent and a child"—not at all unreasonable. Each time this subject guessed wrong, she would change the definition of what constituted a good relation. When she guessed that an instance was "right" and it turned out not to be so, she would explain away the evidence before her: yes, the mother was giving the daughter something in the little scene, but perhaps it was to make up for something bad that had gone before. She interpreted one card as a "rejecting" father face-to-face with a "chastened" son, and upon finding out the card was *not* negative, she said, "Well, confrontation is not always bad, you know."

We, the experimenters, were operating in a paradigmatic world of attributes that constituted instances that met or did not meet criteriality. Our subjects were more often involved in constructing dramatic episodes and looking for kinship and differences between them. When, as we did in some instances, we faced our subjects with what they were doing in contrast to what we had instructed them to do, they protested that we had never said that. They simply were not "processing" the cards in the analytic way that we had expected. They were constructing narratives and, like good literary critics, looking for metaphoric kinship between them.

Again, fallacy? No, I would argue that it was not. It was simply another way of construing the task, of constructing realities, even of building categories. In Wittgenstein's sense, it was a different "form of life."

And so the point I would make in conclusion is a simple one: psychological reality is revealed when a distinction made in one domain—language, modes of organizing human knowledge, whatever—can be shown to have a base in the psychological processes that people use in negotiating their transactions with the world.

7

Nelson Goodman's Worlds

A little over a half-century ago philosophers and psychologists at Harvard shared a single department housed in Emerson Hall, its ground-floor corridor presided over by a seated, slightly frowning Ralph Waldo Emerson in bronze. The psychologists by then could scarcely wait to be free of their old-fashioned parents. That came soon enough. For what had psychology, armed with its shiny new tools of empirical enquiry, to do with metaphysics? Did you need philosophical speculation to study sensation, perception, and behavior? Psychology even then had embraced the physicist Percy Bridgman's "operationalism," a philosophical position holding that scientific concepts, such as mass or "mind," could only be defined by the experimental operations that were used to establish their application to things or processes. Where psychologists were concerned, that was as much philosophy as was needed. IQ, accordingly, was simply what intelligence tests measured. Viennese logical positivism, moreover, defined the line between philosophy and psychology. According to its principles, only statements in science or elsewhere that were true by definition (as in logic or mathematics) or were "empirically verifiable" were meaningful and worthy of study, the former by philosophy and the latter by the sciences, of which psychology was obviously one.

After World War II, psychology and philosophy met principally over "methodology": like the businessman and his accountant, the

This chapter was written with Carol Feldman.

latter told the former the right way to talk about the numbers he had produced. But improving the "language" of academic psychology to conform with the prevailing philosophy of science did little to soften psychology's hard nose. "Mind" remained a forbidden four-letter word in mainstream psychology, to be dealt with (if at all) in quotation marks, whether in voice intonation at symposia or in the inverted commas of print. The "methodology" of "scientific psychology" grew stricter and more puritan by the year; its terms and concepts had to be objectively based, had increasingly to conform to the astringent rules of operational definition. Methods became a preoccupation: methods for making the subjective objective, the hidden overt, the abstract concrete.

Then, in the late 1950s, came what today is called the cognitive revolution. Psychologists like Herbert Simon and George Miller and linguists like Noam Chomsky devoted themselves not to their subjects' overt, objective responses, but rather to what they knew, how they acquired knowledge and used it. The emphasis shifted from performance (what people *did*), to competence (what they *knew*). And this inevitably led to the question of how knowledge was represented in the mind. Could you simulate the mind's knowledge with a computational program (as Simon was attempting to do) or with a theory of mental organization (as Piaget was doing)? "Mind" was being reintroduced into psychology, defined variously as ways in which knowledge was organized, or as a set of strategies for deploying knowledge in order to achieve intended outcomes, and so on. When Simon demonstrated that you could construct computational programs that solved theorems in Whitehead and Russell's *Principia*, or got the missionaries across the river safely in "Cannibals and Missionaries," it was altogether appropriate to ask whether and in what degree these programs were mind-like. And if these programs presupposed that knowledge was represented in the mind, what sorts of representations were these, and what was the mind that contained them? Is that knowledge organized in terms of the specific intentions that dictated its acquisition, or is it all-purpose and general? Moreover, how did we or how did a program representing "us" come by our knowledge of the world? The new questions came in torrents, questions now interesting to the philosopher and psychologist alike.

The new cognitive psychology declared that the choice that guides action is as real as the action that ensues; principles of choice require explanation as a form of mental action. But while overt actions are observable and countable, the thoughts and rules that guide them are not "objective" in this sense. They are mental. And there was the rub. Is a science of thinking not a science until it meets the criteria of objectifiability? Or, to put it another way, was a philosophy of science that demanded such objectifiability the only possible or correct one? Anglo-American philosophy of science, derived from writers like Rudolf Carnap or Carl Hempel, had taken nineteenth-century physics—not psychology—as its exemplar of "good science"; it had insisted that whatever is alleged to exist must be shown to be physical or, at least, reducible to what is physical. But the increased attention among psychologists to cognitive processes—to such unobjectifiable processes as thinking and knowing—challenged this position. So, after more than half a century of independence, psychologists began visiting philosophers on something more than a social basis; the problems that the new psychology posed sat uncomfortably with old philosophy of science, indeed demanded a new philosophy of science.

❧

Nelson Goodman is one of the major philosophers in the world today who addresses himself to the solution of this tangled set of problems. His *Of Mind and Other Matters* takes up where his two earlier books left off, and replies to critics of those earlier books, *Ways of World Making* and *Languages of Art*. (Unless otherwise noted, quotations are from *Of Mind and Other Matters*).

Of Mind and Other Matters defends a "constructivist" philosophy. It is at one blow a philosophy of science, a philosophy of art, and a philosophy of cognition—he ends by calling it "a philosophy of understanding." Its central thesis, "constructivism," is that contrary to common sense there is no unique "real world" that preexists and is independent of human mental activity and human symbolic language; that what we call the world is a product of some mind whose symbolic procedures construct the world. He argues that in some forms of mental functioning, as for example in perception, we already know a great deal about how mental processes operate constructionally: "the overwhelming case against perception without conception, the pure given, absolute immediacy, the innocent eye, substance as substrate, has been so fully and frequently set forth—by Berkeley, Kant, Cassirer, Gombrich, Bruner, and many others—as to need no restatement here" (*WWM*, p. 6). The world of appearance, the very world we live in, is "created" by mind. The activity of world making is, for Goodman, a diverse and complex set of activities, and however else it may express itself it involves "making not with hands but with minds, or rather with languages or other symbol systems" (ibid., p. 42). The worlds we create, he says, may arise from the cognitive activity of the artist (the world of Joyce's *Ulysses*) or in the sciences (whether the geocentric world view of the Middle Ages or that of modern physics), or in ordinary life (as in the commonsense world of trains, cabbages, and kings). Such worlds (he insists) have been constructed, but always out of other worlds, created by others, which we have taken as given. We do not operate on some sort of aboriginal reality independent of our own minds or the minds of those who precede or accompany us.

On Goodman's view, then, no one "world" is more "real" than all others, none is ontologically privileged as the unique real world. In consequence, the physical raw stuff of the physical monist is no more "real" than any other version, and if anything, less real than the psychological processes that created them. The implication of this claim is that the debate between monistic philosophers of science and cognitive psychologists is empty.

❧

The constructivist view, that what exists is a product of what is thought, can be traced to Kant, who first fully developed it. Kant, in turn, attributed his insight to Hume's discovery that certain relations among things in the real world could not be attributed to events but rather were mental constructions projected onto an "objective world." Kant's principal case rested on the relationship of cause and effect. Hume had seen that causation was a mental construct imposed on a mere sequence of events. Kant's view of a world "out there" being made up of mental products is Goodman's starting point.

But as already noted, Goodman refuses to assign any privileged status or any "ultimate reality" to any particular world that mind may create. Kant, on the other hand, argued that we all have certain knowledge, a priori, by virtue of having human minds. Such a priori knowledge, on Kant's view, precedes all reasoning. In place of Kant's a priori, Goodman offers a more relativistic notion. We do not begin with something absolute or prior to all reasoning, but, according to Goodman, begin instead with the kinds of construction that lead to the creation of worlds. And these constructions have in common that they take certain premises for granted, as stipulations. What is "given" or assumed at the outset of our construction is neither bedrock reality out there, nor an a priori: it is always another constructed version of a world that we have taken as given for certain purposes. Any previously constructed world version may be taken as given for subsequent constructions. So, in effect, world making involves the transformation of worlds and world versions already made.

Obviously, the idea of mind as an instrument of construction is (or should be) congenial to the developmental psychologist who observes different meanings being assigned to the same "event" at different ages. The clinical psychologist must always be impressed with the "reality" with which patients endow their rich narratives. And constructivism is nowhere more compelling than in the psychology of art and creativity. Blake, Kafka, Wittgenstein, and Picasso did not find the worlds they produced. They invented them.

Goodman's notion of stipulation—of taking something as given—is also richly suggestive for cognitive psychologists. One immediately thinks of the importance of mechanisms like "recursion," the process whereby the mind or a computer program loops back on the output of a prior computation and treats it as a given that can be the input for the next operation. Theories as divergent as Chomsky's theory of grammar, Piaget's account of the development of mental functions, and Newell and Simon's idea of a General Problem Solver all have recourse to it. Any formal theory of mind is helpless without recursion, for without it it is impossible to account for thoughts on thoughts, thoughts on thoughts on thoughts, up to whatever level of abstraction is necessary. Indeed, Philip Johnson-Laird, in his excellent *Mental Models*, invokes recursion to account for how the mind turns around on itself to create the kind of summary of its capacities that might constitute something like a sense of "self." One begins to get a glimmer from this work of how Goodman's stipulations might be used in sequences, each transforming a previously created world version into a new one, the whole providing a basis for understanding not only single acts of cognition but also complex ones that have the look and smell of real world-making. So far, so good.

It would seem on the surface of it, then, that Goodman would become the immediate idol of cognitive psychologists. But though he has been taken to heart by some, others have been indifferent to his views. It is surely not that psychologists fail to appreciate Goodman's stress on the active role of mind in creating "worlds," nor do most of them doubt that we assign social reality to the pictures of a world we create. But "interpretive social science" of the kind represented, say, by Clifford Geertz in anthropology, emphasizing the irreducibility of meaning, has not had much hearing in psychology. Psychologists (even cognitive psychologists) like to think of worlds that people create as "representing" a real or aboriginal world. Even Piaget, whose epistemological theory was a constructivist one—with more elaborated constructs encompassing simpler ones in the course of growth—clung nonetheless to a residual naive realism. Constructions for him were representations of an autonomous real world to which the growing child had to fit or "accommodate."

Once an aboriginal reality is given up, we lose the criterion of correspondence as a way of distinguishing true from false models of the world. Under these conditions, what can protect us against the galloping relativism that threatens to ensue? (Radical relativism, as we shall see, is as unacceptable to Goodman as it is to his critics.) Goodman's solution begins by distinguishing between versions and worlds. About worlds and world versions, he writes:

> We must obviously look for truth not in the relation of a version to something outside it that it refers to, but in characteristics of the version itself and its relationships to other versions . . . When the world is lost and correspondence along with it, the first thought is usually coherence. But the answer cannot lie in coherence alone; for a false or otherwise wrong version can hold together as well as a right one. Nor do we have any self-evident truths, absolute axioms, unlimited warranties, to distinguish right from among coherent versions; other considerations must enter into that choice. (p. 37)

But what other considerations? Goodman's case rests on the formulation of a criterion (or criteria) adequate to the issue of what makes some world versions right and others not. This is no small order, and Goodman spends much effort trying to fill it.

According to Goodman, there is an irreducible plurality of "worlds." His reason for tolerating a multiplicity of worlds is a principled one: "Some truths conflict. The earth stands still, revolves about the sun, and runs many other courses all at the same time. Yet nothing moves while at rest" (p. 31). How do we escape this contradiction? "Usually," says Goodman,

> we seek refuge in simple-minded relativization: according to a geocentric system the earth stands still, while according to a heliocentric system it moves. But there is no solid comfort here. Merely that a given version says something does not make what it says true; after all, some versions say the earth is flat or that it rests on the back of a tortoise. That the earth is at rest according to one system and moves according to another says nothing about how the earth behaves but only something about what these versions say. What must be added is that these versions are true. (p. 30)

Goodman accommodates these "conflicting truths" by treating them as "versions . . . true in different worlds" (pp. 30–31). Since "there are conflicting true versions and they cannot be true in the same world" (p. 31), there must be many worlds. These worlds do not occupy the same space or time. "In any world," he says, "there is only one Earth" (p. 31); and the several worlds do not risk collision in the same space-time. Indeed, "space-time is an ordering within a world; the space-time of different worlds are not embraced within some greater space-time" (p. 31). These plural worlds cannot be reduced by any maneuver to some single world, even to that of modern physics.

So Goodman's answer lies in drawing a distinction between "worlds" and "versions." He remarks that a "world is not the version itself; the version may have features—such as being in English or consisting of words—that its world does not" (p. 34). Or again, "a version saying that there is a star up there is not itself bright or far off, and the star is not made up of letters" (p. 41). This suggests that versions exist independent of a world they are versions of. On the other hand, he says, "We make versions, and right versions make worlds. And however distinct worlds may be from right versions, making right versions is making worlds" (p. 42). Goodman's answer is obscure: he seems to say both that there is and that there is not a difference between worlds and versions. "Somewhat like the physicist with his field theory and his particle theory, we can have it both ways. To say that every right version is a world and to say that every right version has a world answering to it may be equally right even if they are at odds with each other. Moreover, talk of worlds and talk of right versions are often interchangeable" (pp. 40–41). We can "acknowledge," he says, that a right version and its world are "different." But, he continues, the world in question is not independent of the versions: "The objects themselves and the time and space they occupy are version-dependent. No organization into units is unique or mandatory, nor is there any featureless raw material underlying different organizations. Any raw stuff is as much a creature of a version as is what is made out of that stuff" (p. 41). The decision to speak, on the one hand, of linguistic versions of worlds or, on the other, of worlds themselves (what the versions refer to) becomes for Goodman a matter of practice, of convenience or convention, not a decision about objective fact.

Goodman's canon of convenience and convention, since it does not provide a universal criterion, must remain ambiguous in practice, and it may well, alas, be an ambiguity that is built into any thoroughgoing constructivism. Nevertheless, it is a useful beginning. For, despite its metaphysical ambiguity, his claim that we construct worlds with the help of symbol systems by operating on a "given world" that we take for granted is, from a cognitive point of view, more correct, perhaps, than Goodman himself is prepared to admit when he claims half-mockingly that the distinction between "version" and "world" melts away on close inspection. Interpreted in this way, Goodman's views have powerful consequences for our understanding of such human products as scientific theory, art, and cognitive activity generally.

And that is what much of *Of Mind and Other Matters* is about (as was *Ways of World Making* before it). So we do well to sample Goodman's offerings. Take first his efforts in the philosophy of science. Should one give up physicalism in physics in favor of a thoroughgoing constructivism? As W. V. O. Quine remarked in his review of *Ways of World Making,* physical theory is "ninety-nine parts conceptualization to one part observation," and that makes "nature" a poor candidate for the "real" world. Indeed, the intellectual vigor of modern physics is precisely its sensitivity in choosing appropriate theoretical descriptions to interpret particular observations. Some may claim that because he refuses to call any world or construction more "real" than any other, Goodman cannot capture within his philosophy the widespread belief that the theoretical constructions of modern science are uniquely successful in providing us with mastery over natural events. His pluralism seems to reduce science to the same level as any other "right" construction, whether philosophy or painting. But this is to misinterpret Goodman's intent. What he is urging, rather, is that we ask the hard but inevitable questions about the mental operations required to construct a world like that of modern physics or that of everyday life. And then once physics is "entrenched"—becomes a conventional version—we may ask how it operates within the domain that it has taken as given. This is what Abraham Pais did in his biography of Einstein, what Piaget did for the child's conception of the world, and what Howard Gardner does in his efforts to understand children's drawings.

The same goes for world versions created by the artist, the novelist, the patient in therapy. For Goodman, it will be clear by now, is a philosopher of mind who believes that science and art grow out of certain common constructional activities, guided in each case by different constraints for establishing rightness and different conventions that grow out of their "entrenchment." The difference for him is *not* that the arts are "subjective" and science "objective." Rather, each constructs its world differently, and objectivity versus subjectivity is not the distinction at issue.

What *is* at issue, he proposes, is the difference in the constructional activities of the various arts and sciences, and particularly differences in the use of what he calls "symbol systems." Goodman has devoted a mighty effort to developing a theory of symbols, the most mature expression of which is to be found in his *Languages of Art*. In that book, as in *Mind and Other Matters,* he develops the proposition that "much of knowing, acting, and understanding in the arts, sciences, and life in general involves the use—the interpretation, application, invention, revision—of symbol systems" (p. 152).

The central notion of his theory of symbols is that of "reference." As he puts it, reference is a "primitive term covering all sorts of symbolization, all cases of *standing for*" (p. 55). There are literal and nonliteral modes of reference, with simple and complex forms that provide a range and a subtlety that can be exploited in the world making of both science and art. Even in the case of verbal denotation—naming, describing, predicating, "where a word or a string of words applies to one thing, event, and so on, or to each of many," reference is dependent on context (as with words like *here* and *now*) (p. 55). Indeed, reference may be more or less vague, more or less dependent on the nature of the discourse in which it is embedded. Even in that allegedly simple case of pictorial denotation which has resemblance as its aim, Goodman says: "Resemblance is heavily dependent on custom and culture, so whether and to what extent a symbol is 'iconic,' or faithfully depicts its subject, may vary without any change in the symbol . . ." (p. 57). The meaning of the symbol is given by the system of meanings in which it exists. A line can be the richly descriptive line that represents a hill in a landscape drawing, or the line standing for temperature on a thermometer in a sparse system that lacks this repleteness.

Each system of symbols has its referential properties: fictive, figurative, and metaphoric denotations alter the referential distance they impose between a symbol and what it stands for. Hieronymus Bosch's *Garden of Earthly Delights* manages in its mode of depiction to be both fantastic and realistic. Both what is told and the mode of telling enter into our conception of what a work of art is about. Wherever one looks at the creation of realities, we see the complexity of symbol systems, the dependence of what they create on the discourse on which they are set and on the purposes to which the creation is to be put. Each symbol system is a means for transforming whatever stipulative givens (themselves expressed in a symbol system) that system accepts as input. Studying how this is done in such diverse domains as painting and literary interpretation and science is Goodman's recommended agenda for the philosopher, an agenda he proposes should supplant work on the false ideal of comparing works of art or science to a "real" world for their "truth" or "distortion."

❧

In the two earlier books *Ways of World Making* and *The Languages of Art,* Goodman goes to some pains to explicate some of the "larger-scale" ways in which worlds are made from previous versions. We compose and decompose worlds, impelled by different aims in doing so—practical as well as theoretical, now emphasizing constituent, now contingent features in our constructions. We weight and emphasize features of previous worlds in creating new ones, and "what counts as emphasis, of course, is departure from the relative prominence of the several features in the current world of our everyday seeing" (*WWM,* p. 11). We impose order, and since all is in motion, the order or reordering we impose is a way too of imposing alternate stabilities. We delete and supplement and condemn to nonreality everything that exists between C and C#. We deform the given that we took, and create caricature, the caricature itself being principled rather than entirely fanciful. And we do it not only in art but in science. There is, for example, a famous "map" popularized by the physiologist Lord Adrian in his *The Basis of Sensation*, depicting the monkey with each part of the body enlarged to correspond to its density of sensory innervation—its lips and tongue in this caricature grossly larger than its trunk and torso.

Goodman believes that there are practical consequences to the practice of philosophy, consequences particularly for the conduct of the arts and the sciences, and even for the way we conduct our educational process. But he doubts that philosophers acting alone could get very far with these practical matters. In consequence, Goodman as much as any modern philosopher makes common intellectual cause with artists, psychologists, film makers. In 1967 he founded Project Zero at the Graduate School of Education at Harvard, and there, together with others from a wide variety of backgrounds, he has engaged in research on education for the arts. And there is no question that his philosophical views have had an impact on a generation of students of the creative process in the arts as well as in the cognitive processes generally. Howard Gardner's *Frames of Mind* is a good case in point, for Gardner has been associated with Project Zero from the start and now directs it. Gardner's effort to characterize the different modes of operation by which intelligence expresses itself is deeply in the Goodmanian tradition. Characteristically, its central claim is that minds become specialized to deal in verbal or mathematical or spatial forms of world making, supported by symbolic means provided by cultures which themselves specialize in their preference for different kinds of worlds.

Goodman puts the case well for the relevance of his views for the cognitive analysis of world making through the arts:

> "Cognitive" has been a battle cry in psychology and philosophy of the arts for some decades. The movement it stands for, one of the most liberating and productive in this century, is often decried by behavioristically oriented theorists as nonempirical and unscientific, and widely thought by writers on art to be bent on analysing the arts to death.
>
> The trouble arises, I think, from a complex of confusions: confusion about cognition, about education, and about art and science. The cognitive approach to education for the arts must surely be condemned if cognition is contrasted with perception, emotion, and all nonlogical and

> nonlinguistic faculties; or if education is identified exclusively with lecturing, explaining, and providing texts and verbal and numerical exercises; or if art is looked upon as transient amusement for a passive audience, while science is taken as consisting of demonstrations founded upon observation and aimed at practical progress . . . Cognition includes learning, knowing, gaining insight and understanding by all available means . . . Coming to understand a painting or a symphony in an unfamiliar style, to recognize the work of an artist or school, to see or to hear in new ways, is as cognitive an achievement as learning to read or write or add . . .
>
> The genuine and significant differences between art and science are compatible with their common cognitive function; and the philosophy of science and the philosophy of art are embraced within epistemology conceived as the philosophy of understanding . . . Since both science and art consist very largely in the processing of symbols, an analysis and classification of types of symbol systems . . . provides an indispensable theoretical background (for them both). (pp. 146–147)

So one comes to the conclusion that Goodman's work is, in effect, a very serious effort to create, as he puts it, a philosophy of understanding. But it is a philosophy of understanding that is so pluralistic that its worth cannot be assessed fairly without considering its power over the many particular worlds to which it relates—the analysis of painting, of visual apparent movement, of the ordering in pictorial narrative, of the structure of linguistic systems, of the creation of fictions like Don Quixote or postulational systems for defining points in space. After all, if reality is what one stipulates (rather than finds), the range of stipulation is great, and what one makes of what one has stipulated is not something to be determined by quick intuition.

❧

So whatever the limitations of Goodman's proposals, he has made clearer a concept of mind to be specified not in terms of properties but rather as an instrument for producing worlds. His point of view has obviously had a strong influence in the preceding chapters of this book and will in later ones. Psychologists, as we have noted, have had a struggle with the central epistemological question that he raises. For psychology, by inheritance, given that the psychophysicists Gustave Fechner and Wilhelm Wundt were its founding fathers, felt that it had to take a stand on how mind and its mental processes transform the physical world through operations on input. The moment one abandons the idea that "the world" is there once for all and immutably, and substitutes for it the idea that what we take as the world is itself no more nor less than a stipulation couched in a symbol system, then the shape of the discipline alters radically. And we are, at last, in a position to deal with the myriad forms that reality can take—including the realities created by story, as well as those created by science.

8

Thought and Emotion

In an earlier chapter, I decried the habit of drawing heavy conceptual boundaries between thought, action, and emotion as "regions" of the mind, then later being forced to construct conceptual bridges to connect what should never have been put asunder. I propose now to pursue that argument further.

Only two of the terms in the classical triad are in the title of this chapter—even two make the task daunting enough. Besides, I want to argue that actions (anticipated, in progress, and recalled) infuse our representations of the world. Conceiving of a possible world includes conceiving of procedures for operating upon it. To put it in Edward Tolman's slightly archaic language, a cognitive map of a domain includes means-end readinesses for acting within it, else we would have a theory that "left the animal wrapt in thought."

Take first the concept of thought. It is, to begin with, a highly refined abstraction, an abstraction originally formulated in philosophy precisely to contrast it with activity governed by unreason and "tainted by passion." The defining character of thought is its product: the outcome of pure thought always passed the test of right reason. What did not conform was not, in the strict sense, pure thought. It was no accident that the mathematician George Boole entitled his famous work on algebra *The Laws of Thought*. Thought, in this dispensation, is a normative idea, a specification of a criterion of right reason. I want to call this the Classical Abstraction. If this Classical Abstraction had worked, the intersect between thought and emotion would constitute a null class. I am not intending only a logical joke, for it was certainly the hope of early logicians and philosophers to find some way of sorting out the chaff of unreason from the wheat of reason. And this was to be accomplished by the provision of finer and finer rules of right reason (that is, laws of logic) rather than by closer and closer description of the activity of thinking itself (or, for that matter, of emotion).

Unfortunately, there was a problem that obtruded. There were "errors" in reasoning that had to be taken account of. These errors were, in effect, departures from the rules of right reason, and it is interesting to note how much time was spent by classical and medieval logicians in specifying the *nature* of these errors. They were labeled and botanized, and, indeed, they are part of our logical heritage even today. What student of introductory logic does not know the misuses of *modus tollens* and *modus ponens*?

It is curious how little psychological curiosity there was about the sources of these errors, and from the Sophists to Würzburg one can find relatively little difference in the way they were accounted for. They were "weaknesses" in our logical processes, earlier couched in terms of weaknesses for the undistributed middle, later as "set effects" or "atmosphere effects." To put it in a word, there was no *psychology* of thought, only logic and a catalogue of logical errors. Insofar as anybody ventured a psychological idea on the subject, it was to remark that our "weaknesses" in doing logic might on occasion be fed by our biases and our passions, that if a wrong conclusion to a syllogism went the way of our biases, we would be more likely to offer it or to accept it.

The same case holds for the history of inference as for deduction, as with the "base rate fallacy" I discussed in Chapter 6. Departure from Bayesian criteria is "fallacy," and departures, as before, are attributed to weakness, some to weakness induced by bias.

As always in the history of ideas, of course, there is another side of the coin. With the establishment of medieval schools of learning, logic was joined in a common faculty with grammar and rhetoric to constitute the Trivium. While the logicians were making a virtual catalogue of "logical errors," the rhetoricians were studying the ways (if I may be permitted a certain historical license) of trapping people into those errors—not really, of course, but the rhetoricians' devices of argument were in fact that. And recall too, as Father Walter Ong always reminds us, that learned discourse throughout that period (and indeed into the nineteenth century) was conducted *viva voce* in oratorical strophes and was not confined to the dusty pages of learned journals. So the opportunities for (if I may so put it) "swaying the emotions" of the listener were many and were carefully cultivated.

One other overwhelmingly important distinction has marked the history of our topic. In the theological debates of the Schoolmen, debates that shaped conceptions not only of the nature of God but also of man and his mind, there was a sharp distinction drawn between faith and reason, the one guided by revelation and the other by logic or the rules of "right reason." If one reads the works of Werner Jaeger and of Harry Wolfson on the Patristic philosophers, it soon becomes plain that two forms of knowing (if I may use those secular terms) were taken for granted, two forms of knowing that long before had become established in classical Greece. One was an unmediated knowing of eternal truths revealed by God (or, in Plato, by virtue of man's endowment with an intuition of pure knowledge). It was revelation. The other was through observation and the application of logic to what had been observed. And of course, it was the failure to distinguish sharply between the analytic and synthetic aspects of the latter mode that led to the confusion between deductive and empirical science that prevailed until Francis Bacon. But the crucial distinction historically was between Faith and Reason.

The struggle between the two in the minds of man was, most certainly, the core of the intellectual drama of the Middle Ages. Etienne Gilson, in *Reason and Revelation in the Renaissance,* argues that the dynamic of the Renaissance lay in the achievement of a new balance between the former and the latter. Faced with a conflict between Reason and Faith, the religious man had no option but to follow the latter. And indeed, it is upon the elaboration of that theme that St. Augustine's *Confessions* is based.

All of which is not to say that the two were all. There were also Folly, and above all, Sin. Folly issued from a failure to conduct oneself in the light of reason; Sin from violating ethical tenets that were known through Faith.

By the time of the Enlightenment, then, the topics of thought and emotion were as theological as they were psychological. When Descartes wrote the *Discourse on Method*, his "principle of doubt" could be taken (and was taken) as an attack on religious faith rather than as a guideline in a projected science of inquiry. And to this day, the topic of "thought and emotion" remains clouded. For though Western society has become increasingly secularized since the Enlightenment, a secularization hastened by the Industrial Revolution and its sequelae, there always remain vestiges of the ancient distinction, if only in the recurrences of romanticism and in revivals of religious faith, both spontaneous and politically inspired.

So our topic is not an easy one to look at "in the cool light of reason," for that cool light is often the very point at issue, though it is most often a concealed issue. What I propose to do in the pages following is to explore how we might conceive of thought and emotion and their relationship in the light of the constructivist position that I have been trying to set forth in this book.

❧

We know the world in different ways, from different stances, and each of the ways in which we know it produces different structures or representations, or, indeed, "realities." As we grow to adulthood (at least in Western culture), we become increasingly adept at seeing the same set of events from *multiple* perspectives or stances and at entertaining the results as, so to speak, alternative possible worlds. The child, we would all agree, is less adept at achieving such multiple perspectives—although it is highly dubious, as we have already seen in Chapter 4, that children are as uniformly egocentric as formerly claimed. There is every reason to insist, as I tried to do in that chapter, that the human capacity for taking multiple perspectives must be present in some workable form in order for the child to master language. And within each of the perspectives the child can take (or the adult can take) she is capable of imposing principles of organization that have an internal "logic" in the sense of being principled rather than simply producing results conforming to "right reason." It was to Piaget's everlasting credit to demonstrate that an internal logic guided the young child much as it did the scientist, and that both could be shown to adhere to a principled set of operations.

A generation of research extending from the New Look through contemporary studies in filtering and information processing, however, tells us that each mode of representing the world carries with it a prescription as to what is "acceptable" as input: experience, so to speak, is not "theory-independent." The limits of our processing system, whatever mode of organizing is operative, impose still further selectivity on input as well as on the interpretation of input. As Robert Woodworth put it half a century ago, there is no seeing without looking, no hearing without listening, and both looking and listening are shaped by expectancy, stance, and intention.

Add to this one further cultural point. We give different "reality" status to experiences we create from our differently formed encounters with the world. We place a canonical value on certain stances that yield certain forms of knowledge, certain possible worlds. One such stance is the "scientific" or "rational" or "logical" one. For it yields accounts of experience that are replicable, interpersonally amenable to calibration and easy correction. But much of experience is not of this order. We do not steadily rely on that mode of organizing experience. As John Austin noted two decades ago, the greater part of human discourse is not in the form of either verifiable analytic or synthetic propositions. We deal as well with constitutive realities having to do with requests, promises, affiliations, threats, encouragements, and the like. We even create bricks-and-mortar realities like jails to deal with people who fail to conform to the felicity conditions on certain forms of promising.

On this reasoning, each way of creating and experiencing a world must be regarded in some nontrivial way as the extension of some stance—and some of these stances we call "emotional," while others escape this label. The danger, of course, is that the stances that we consider rational (given the power of the Classical Abstraction in folk psychology) are likely to be viewed as stanceless, as if automatically guided by a ghost in the machine called "right reason." But suppose, by way of self-therapy, we substitute the word "passionate" for "emotional." Then we would perhaps be less willing to draw the old distinction, for example, we would cheerfully say that Immanuel Kant, the Sage of Königsberg, was as "passionate" in his employment of the stance of "right reason" while writing the *Critiques* as Stavrogin was devoted to his obsession in Dostoevski's novel. Both are victims or beneficiaries of selectivity, both are single-minded.

Yet, we would still say that one is "out of control," the other not, and it is a distinction that even the law recognizes: a plan to kill another with due deliberation aforethought is distinguished from a *crime passionelle*. By this criterion "emotion" is freed from its association with *intense* striving and associated with such striving only when it is out of control. It has a commonsense ring of rightness about it: emotion is aroused when a way of construing the world goes out of control. If we take "out of control" to mean not "subject to correction" by input, then the psychological literature has something to say about it. It is an idea embodied in the Yerkes-Dodson Law. The first part of that law states that the stronger the drive, up to a point, the faster learning will be. But beyond that point, increased drive will make an organism "go out of control" and will slow down learning. (The second part of the law is that the more complex the task, the less the amount of drive needed to achieve the maximum point on the U-shaped curve. Perhaps that is why Kant took forty years, or so it is said, to complete the *Critique of Pure Reason*!)

In a word, the effect of too much drive is to create a state that disrupts or otherwise interferes with effective cognition. Suppose we provisionally label this state "emotion." We can admit immediately that it is far too crude a way either of characterizing emotion (what of tender feelings?) or of specifying the conditions that create it (surely emotions are not associated *only* with being out of control). Yet it is an interesting step in pursuit of our question of how cognition and emotion interact. Let us pursue it a bit further.

Two examples from the research literature will help, both of them from the study of rat learning, where the issues are clearer even if they are reminiscent of the half-crown in the Chesterton story, which the Irishman searches for under the street lamp because that is where the light is. At least they will help specify more clearly what might be meant by being "out of control."

In the first example, the issue is what is called Vicarious Trial and Error (VTE for short), which was taken by cognitive learning theorists of the 1950s as an animal *Anlage* of consciousness. It was measured principally by counting the number of times that an animal in a maze paused at a choice point to look back and forth between the alternative routes or between possible "signposts" or cues. Those who have spent time playing the specialized chess of rat research will recognize the metaphoric rightness of this measure, introduced by Karl Muenzinger a generation ago. (Even B. F. Skinner, never sympathetic to cognitive concepts, had to introduce some version of the idea into his system of thinking, calling it the "observing response" and remarking on its intractability to ordinary schedules of reinforcement.) What is remarkable about VTE is that it most often occurs on trials in the maze immediately preceding correct solution, as if marking when the rats start paying close attention. Muenzinger found that the more driven the animals were by severe hunger (that is, the longer they had been deprived of food beyond a certain optimal point before testing), the less VTE they exhibited. "Overdrive" cuts down scanning or observing; "emotion" reduces the uptake of cues.

A later experiment (by Bruner, Matter, and Papanek) added to that finding. This time there were two sets of cues at each choice point in the maze, two completely redundant ones, either or both of which could be used to steer the animal toward the food box at the end of the maze. One was a "spatial" cue: the correct door at each of the choice points was arranged in an alternating pattern (Left-Right-Left-Right), which is a rather "highbrow" pattern for rats to learn. The other was provided by the color of the doors at each choice point: the darker of the two gray doors was the correct one.

Again, there were two groups of rats, one on a reasonable schedule of food deprivation, the other very hungry. (The hungrier animals, by the way, *acted* more emotionally: they were jumpier, were more likely to defecate when they encountered a blocked door, and the like.) Which animals, en route to learning the maze, would have noticed the dual set of cues? As expected, the moderately hungry ones. Take away the brightness marking on the doors by painting them both middle gray, and the highly driven animals (though they could run the maze by following the visual cues) fell back to near random choosing. The moderately hungry animals paused briefly when the visual signposts were removed, and then proceeded to use the alternative single-alternation pattern to get to the food at the end of the maze. And so it would seem that emotional state not only cuts down the amount of sheer looking but also makes what looking there is narrower or more specialized or more "primitive" (in the sense that the visual signposts were more immediate).

So let us sum up the argument thus far. As it has proceeded, the general question about "emotion and thought" has become more specific. On the one side, we can specify amount of drive in excess of what is required to keep the organism at the task (according to the Yerkes-Dodson Law). On the other, we can specify something about the reduction of uptake under such conditions, and even say something about its "narrowness" or "single-mindedness." That is some progress—even if it has to be earned by reference to rats. It has, moreover, a certain elegance as a formulation. It suggests a law of economy of functioning based on a trade-off principle: when need is high, the time given to information processing declines and the depth of that processing declines. Preoccupation with the goal smothers occupation with the means to it.

Immediately one is tempted to find "parallels" in higher creatures like man. Like an analyst's case report I once heard. The patient, upon entering the consulting room, looked all about him and commented that the furniture had been rearranged, but that he couldn't figure out how. The analyst suggested he take a closer look at her, which he did. Even then, he failed to notice that she was sporting a full-blown black eye. The patient, the reader will not be surprised to learn, was in the midst of working out his very hostile feelings toward his analyst, which he resisted admitting, as he was then also resisting admitting hostility toward the cold and rejecting mother of his childhood. Can the idea of "narrowing" of input be extended to the patient's blocking out his analyst's shiner? The metaphor groans pretty hard.

Yet, there are some simple, probably biologically based linkages between emotion, arousal, drive on the one side, and learning, problem solving, thinking on the other. And they seem fruitful to pursue (even in the light of more sophisticated accounts of emotion, such as those offered by Silvan Tomkins). And linkages of the kinds I have been discussing do bear upon the question of how we construct and construe the worlds in which we operate. But what is lacking, of course, is an account of how symbolic activity, so crucial to a constructivist's view of "world making," enters the scene.

❧

Let me approach the matter from the perspective of development, particularly in the light of what we know about language acquisition in children.

Obviously children quickly and painlessly master syntax without crisis. With somewhat more difficulty, but still easily, the child also "learns how to mean"—how to refer to the world with sense. But children do not master syntax for its own sake or learn how to mean simply as an intellectual exercise—like little scholars or lexicographers. They acquire these skills in the interest of getting things done in the world: requesting, indicating, affiliating, protesting, asserting, possessing, and the rest. These are familiar matters visited in earlier chapters.

It is quite plain that the simpler "uses" of communication develop before language proper comes on the scene. Requesting, indicating, affiliating are realized by gesture, by vocalization, by "body language," by regulation of gaze before lexico-grammatical speech appears. When it does appear, it is used for perfecting, differentiating, and extending these functions. Eventually, the child learns to perform certain speech acts that can be performed *only* by the use of language proper, the typical example being promising. These are the performatives that so caught the imagination of philosophers and anthropologists in the 1960s and after. For performatives operate by creating social realities.

These realities, these constructed social contexts, provide the "signature" for emotional states. That is to say, to choose a very obvious example, being faced with a broken promise produces shame in a manner that can be recognized by the person who feels it as related to "promise-breaking." But neither the phenomenon of *breaking a promise* not its affective counterpart of *shame* could occur were it not for the constitutive power of a speech act to create its social reality. Put simply, emotions achieve their qualitative character by being contextualized in the social reality that produces them.

I want now to offer an hypothesis as to how, in the course of development, this contextualizing, or signaturizing, of emotion is brought about.

We already know from Sperber and Wilson that listeners to language almost always operate on the assumption that the speaker is intending to communicate something. It is irresistible, it would seem. Aidan Macfarlane's observations on mothers' talk to infants brought to them for the first time after delivery underlines this irresistibility. His recordings are laced with, "What's that frown for? The world a little surprising, you trying to tell me?" Mothers will tell you that they don't *really* believe the baby understands. But they go on talking that way in spite of what they say. They assign meanings to what their infants are doing, and respond accordingly. And in time, as we have seen, they create formats of interaction, jointly constructed little worlds in which they interact according to the social realities that they have created in their exchanges. This is the child's first "culture." And it is constrained by mutual expectancies which, if they fail to materialize, produce emotional upset. That it is an emotional place, this intimate world, is testified to by a research finding of Alan Sroufe's: those things the parent does that are most likely to produce laughter in the child are the very things likely to produce tears when done by a stranger.

Initiation into family culture is greatly aided by what Daniel Stern has called "attunement." The child's world and the world of his caretaker achieve a working correspondence, and even on a moment-to-moment basis, the two can be observed to be responding to each other in a mutually reinforcing, mutually confirming way. It is the child's happy time. With conflict, attunement is disrupted, and it is unhappy time. Emotion, during the first year of life, seems to be an accompaniment to attunement and its disruption. It is not notably differentiated in a qualitative sense. The child is either happy or unhappy, with some middle arousal state of alert attention and another drowsy state of sleep when he withdraws. (I am not leaving aside the effects of physical discomfort and pain; they are also "emotions." I would only remind the reader that most mothers report that by the eighth or ninth week these recede and their place is taken by what mothers, according to Christopher Pratt, describe as psychological "needs.")

Attunement leads to the happy state, its breach to the unhappy one. Both reflect the degree of fit of the young child's expectations to the ways in which others are responding to him. In time, the child constructs representations of the world that he expects in different situations, constructs them from the encounters he has with those around him, his immediate "culture." Emotion then begins to take on a qualitative character that relates to situations, and the mother is able correctly to tell whether the infant is hungry, frustrated by a toy, lonely, and so on. And she is then able to respond accordingly (or not).

The only problem posed by the child's success in finding the world in attunement with his expectancies is boredom, but that need not concern us. His happiness is assured by providing sufficient variation to prevent boredom—as parents know.

There are subtle cues provided the child with respect to how he is supposed to "feel" in a given situation, particularly in those formatted or ritual situations to which I referred in earlier chapters. You are supposed to feel "grief" when a kinsman dies more than when a stranger dies, "indignation" when somebody infringes your role rights, "delight" when grandparents arrive. If the child fails to pick up these cues, he is (if only unintentionally) "punished" by a breach in attunement or, under better circumstances, he is given a fuller explanation of what the situation is about and what is expected from him. In most cases, if the child does not conform to expectancy about appropriate emotions, the matter becomes one for negotiation, for talk, for illuminating story, and eventually for therapy.

In time, and with sufficient exposure to cues and models, children, in fact, do usually "shape up." But the shaping in question is not usually a matter of calling up some prepared emotion, but consists, rather, of helping the child to contextualize initially undifferentiated feelings into highly differentiated social situations that give these feelings their affective signature.

All of which is not to argue that there is no differentiation in emotional state save that which is given by the socially defined situation in which it occurs. Such a view would be an odd variant of the James-Lange theory that claimed that we are afraid only because we flee. The cultural variant of the James-Lange theory would say that we feel afraid not because we flee but because we recognize that we are in a situation that is culturally defined as dangerous. But such an extreme variant is not necessary. The general view proposed here would hold equally well even if we granted that there were primary or "primitive" emotions like fear, rage, hunger, and sexual arousal, or that each major drive system had its accompanying distinguishable emotion. If that were so (and I do not wish to exclude the possibility), it would still be the case that on our view a more specific affective "signature" would be required. Socially defined context would then serve the role of providing this "signature."

There is certainly evidence in the psychological literature on emotion that supports the view suggested here. One source of it is cross-cultural. Vladimir Bogoraz's observations of the Chukchee provide an early example. These are tundra dwelling people in the far northeast of Russia. Bogoras observed that in Chukchee society strange objects from outside the culture are defined as "disgusting" and produce a nausea reaction. They are presented to children as objects of disgust. But perhaps the strongest evidence for the social contextualization of emotion is to be found in the sexual sphere. Anthropological observations agree on one crucial point. The prescription of exogamy has a powerful shaping effect on sexual arousal, even though it is, so to speak, classificatory (related to categories of males and females rather than to specific persons). Whether a potential partner is *seen* as sexually attractive or not will depend upon how he or she is categorized with respect to the exogamy taboo.

And within our own culture (or any culture), there are certain emotions (like shame, which I considered at the outset of this discussion) that can be defined only in terms of such symbolic systems as kinship, social class, and reference group. Embarrassment (so prominent a feature of adolescent life at the point where childish patterns are being exchanged for adult ones) is a striking case in point. But it too has an adult version that is related to social class. There is a higher incidence of embarrassment toward others whom one defines as above one in social class—and the more so, the more one is socially mobile.

And finally, there is evidence from studies of the effects of adrenalin introduced directly into the bloodstream. How one "feels" in reaction to the hormone is principally determined by the nature of the situation in which one finds (or defines) oneself—whether one is angry, sad, elated, or something else.

There are two ways of drawing conclusions from such data as these. The first, psychological, is that emotional reactions "condition" easily to situational stimuli. And the evidence from conventional studies of emotional conditioning would support that view. There is another approach, however, that does not contradict the first but asks not about the "mechanism," whether conditioning or not, but about the nature of those "situational stimuli" to which conditioning occurs. What are they, and how are they related to one another? The answer is that they are usually not "stimuli" in any Pavlovian sense, but achieve their significance by virtue of being caught in a connected symbol system that constitutes culture.

As such, to go back to the beginning of the argument, the components of the behavior I am speaking of are not emotions, cognitions, and actions, each in isolation, but aspects of a larger whole that achieves its integration only within a cultural system. Emotion is not usefully isolated from the knowledge of the situation that arouses it. Cognition is not a form of pure knowing to which emotion is added (whether to perturb its clarity or not). And action is a final common path based on what one knows and feels. Indeed, our actions are frequently dedicated to keeping a state of knowledge from being upset (as in "autistic hostility") or to the avoidance of situations that are anticipated to be emotion-arousing.

It seems far more useful to recognize at the start that all three terms represent abstractions, abstractions that have a high theoretical cost. The price we pay for such abstractions in the end is to lose sight of their structural interdependence. At whatever level we look, however detailed the analysis, the three are constituents of a unified whole. To isolate each is like studying the planes of a crystal separately, losing sight of the crystal that gives them being.

Part Three

Acting in Constructed Worlds

9

The Language of Education

We are living through bewildering times where the conduct of education is concerned. There are deep problems that stem from many origins—principally from a changing society whose future shape we cannot foresee and for which it is difficult to prepare a new generation.

My topic, the language of education, may seem remote from the bewildering problems that rapid and turbulent change in our society have produced. But I shall try to show before I am done that it is not really so, that it is not so much scholarly fiddling while Rome burns to try to find a key to this crisis in the language of education. For at the heart of any social change one often finds fundamental changes in regard to our conceptions of knowledge and thought and learning, changes whose fulfillment is impeded and distorted by the way in which we talk about the world and think about it in the coin of that talk. My hope is that we may uncover some vexing issues of immediate and practical concern.

I shall begin with a premise that is already familiar: that the medium of exchange in which education is conducted—language—can never be neutral, that it imposes a point of view not only about the world to which it refers but toward the use of mind in respect of this world. Language necessarily imposes a perspective in which things are viewed and a stance toward what we view. It is not just, in the shopworn phrase, that the medium is the message. The message itself may create the reality that the message embodies and predispose those who hear it to think about it in a particular mode. If I had to choose a motto for what I have to say, it would be that one from Francis Bacon, used by Vygotsky, proclaiming that neither mind alone nor hand alone can accomplish much without the aids and tools that perfect them. And principal among those aids and tools are language and the canons of its use.

Most of our encounters with the world are not, as we have seen, direct encounters. Even our direct experiences, so called, are assigned for interpretation to ideas about cause and consequence, and the world that emerges for us is a conceptual world. When we are puzzled about what we encounter, we renegotiate its meaning in a manner that is concordant with what those around us believe.

If this is the basis for our understanding of the physical and biological worlds, how much truer it is of the social world in which we live. For, to sound another familiar theme, the "realities" of the society and of social life are themselves most often products of linguistic use as represented in such speech acts as promising, abjuring, legitimizing, christening, and so on. Once one takes the view that a culture itself comprises an ambiguous text that is constantly in need of interpretation by those who participate in it, then the constitutive role of language in creating social reality becomes a topic of practical concern.

So if one asks the question, where is the meaning of social concepts—in the world, in the meaner's head, or in interpersonal negotiation—one is compelled to answer that it is the last of these. Meaning is what we can agree upon or at least accept as a working basis for seeking agreement about the concept at hand. If one is arguing about social "realities" like democracy or equity or even gross national product, the reality is not the thing, not in the head, but in the act of arguing and negotiating about the meaning of such concepts. Social realities are not bricks that we trip over or bruise ourselves on when we kick at them, but the meanings that we achieve by the sharing of human cognitions.

❧

A negotiatory or "hermeneutic" or transactional view of the kind I have been setting forth has deep and direct implications for the conduct of education. Let me try to state some of these in general terms and then to echo them in terms of more specific and practical matters concerned with schools and teaching.

The most general implication is that a culture is constantly in process of being recreated as it is interpreted and renegotiated by its members. In this view, a culture is as much a *forum* for negotiating and renegotiating meaning and for explicating action as it is a set of rules or specifications for action. Indeed, every culture maintains specialized institutions or occasions for intensifying this "forum-like" feature. Storytelling, theater, science, even jurisprudence are all techniques for intensifying this function—ways of exploring possible worlds out of the context of immediate need. Education is (or should be) one of the principal forums for performing this function—though it is often timid in doing so. It is the forum aspect of a culture that gives its participants a role in constantly making and remaking the culture—an *active* role as participants rather than as performing spectators who play out their canonical roles according to rule when the appropriate cues occur.

Perhaps there have been societies, at least for certain periods of time, that were "classically" traditional and in which one "derived" one's actions from a set of more or less fixed rules. I recall reading, almost with the pleasure one has in watching formal ballet, Marcel Granet's celebrated account of the classic Chinese family. The roles and obligations were as clearly and closely specified as the traditional Bolshoi choreography. But then I had the good fortune to become acquainted at the same time with John Fairbank's account of the extraordinary ease with which, in Chinese warlord politics, legitimacy and loyalty passed to the victor in the local politics of force, by whatever ghastliness victory had been won. I found myself concluding that "equilibrium" accounts of cultures are useful principally to guide the writing of older-style ethnographies or as political instruments for use by those in power to subjugate psychologically whose who must be ruled.

It follows from this view of culture as a forum that induction into the culture through education, if it is to prepare the young for life as lived, should also partake of the spirit of a forum, of negotiation, of the recreating of meaning. But this conclusion runs counter to traditions of pedagogy that derive from another time, another interpretation of culture, another conception of authority—one that looked at the process of education as a *transmission* of knowledge and values *by* those who knew more *to* those who knew less and knew it less expertly. And at another level, it also rested on some presuppositions about the young as underprovided not only epistemically but deontically as well—lacking in a sense of value propositions and a sense of the society. The young were not only underequipped with knowledge about the world, which needed to be imparted to them, but were also "lacking" in values. Their deficit has been variously accounted for psychologically, most of the secular theories being quite as compelling in their way as the earlier divine theories of Original Sin. In our time, for example, we have had theories of primary process based on the axiom that immaturity rests on an incapacity to delay gratification. Or, on the cognitive side, we have had the doctrine of egocentrism, which posited a lack of capacity to see the world from any perspective other than the one in which the child occupies the position of central planet around which all else revolves.

I do not wish to argue against any of these characterizations of the child, whether driven by Original Sin, by primary process, or by egocentrism. Let us assume that, in one degree or another, they are all "right." That is to say, they are "right versions" (in Nelson Goodman's sense) of the world of givens from which they take their start. So long as they begin with those givens and remain consistent with them, they cannot be faulted. But the point I want to make is not about their abstract truth but about their force as ideas shaping educational practice. All of them imply that there should be something rooted out, replaced or compensated. The pedagogy that resulted was some view of teaching as surgery, suppression, replacement, deficit filling, or some mix of them all. When "learning theory" emerged in this century, there was added to the list a further "method," reinforcement: reward and punishment could become the levers of a new technology for accomplishing these ends.

Obviously there have been other voices, other "world versions," and in this last generation they have swelled to a new and powerful chorus. But they have been, in the main, focused on the learning child and his needs as an autonomous learner—an extraordinarily important emphasis. Freud's was among them, particularly his emphasis upon the autonomy of ego functioning and the achievement of freedom from excessive or conflicted drives. And surely Piaget must be counted a major force in this emphasis on learning as invention. What we still lack is a reasoned theory of how the negotiation of meaning as socially arrived at is to be interpreted as a pedagogical axiom, though there has been a beginning in the work of Vygotsky (as is seen in Chapter 5), and in some contemporary theories like those of Michael Cole and Hugh Mehan. I shall come to them presently, but let me see first whether I can clear some preliminary ground.

❧

We need to turn back again to the functions of language, for they are central to the argument. Perhaps Michael Halliday provides the most complete catalogue. He divides functions into two superordinate classes—*pragmatic* and *mathetic*. In the former are such functions as the instrumental, regulatory, interactional, and personal, and to the mathetic he assigns the heuristic, imaginative, and informative functions. We need not unpack these in detail but note only that the class of pragmatic functions are concerned with orienting oneself toward others and using the tool of language to obtain the ends one seeks through affecting the actions and attitudes of others toward oneself and toward the world. The ensemble of mathetic functions serves a different order of function. The heuristic is the means for gaining information and correction from others; the imaginative function is the means whereby we create possible worlds and go beyond the immediately referential. The informative function is constructed on a base of intersubjective presupposition: that somebody has knowledge that I do not possess or that I have knowledge they do not possess, and that such imbalance can be dealt with by any act of talking or "telling." There is perhaps one function, one originally elaborated by Roman Jakobson, that needs to be added to Halliday's list—the metalinguistic function, or turning around on one's use of language to examine or explicate it, as in the analytic mode of philosophers or linguists who look at expressions as if they were, so to speak, opaque objects to be examined in their own right rather than transparent windows through which we look out upon the world.

These functions provide us with useful tools for examining the language of education. Halliday remarks that it is the genius of lexicogrammatical language that it permits and requires the fulfilling of all of these functions simultaneously. They are inescapable. Even using the "unmarked" (or ritual zero) value of one of them marks a stance of the speaker toward the event being represented, toward the occasion of the utterance, and toward the manner in which the speaker expects the listener to view the world and use his mind. It is a subject that I have explored in earlier chapters in discussing such "devices" as implicature, presuppositional triggering, and the imposition of perspective on scenes.

Let me give an example of stance in teacher talk, one drawn from Carol Feldman's work. She was interested in the extent to which teachers' stances toward their subject indicate some sense of the hypothetical nature of knowledge, its uncertainty, its invitation to further thought. She chose as an index the use of modal auxiliary markers in teachers' talk to students and in their talk to each other in the staff room, distinguishing between expressions that contained modals of uncertainty and probability (like *might, could,* and so on) and expressions not so marked. Modals expressing a stance of uncertainty or doubt in teacher talk to teachers far outnumbered their occurrence in teacher talk to students. The world that the teachers were presenting to their students was a far more settled, far less hypothetical, far less negotiatory world than the one they were offering to their colleagues.

Stance marking in the speech of others gives us a clue about how to use our minds. I recall a teacher, her name was Miss Orcutt, who made the statement in class, "It is a very puzzling thing not that water turns to ice at 32 degrees Fahrenheit, but that it should change from a liquid into a solid." She then went on to give us an intuitive account of Brownian movement and of molecules, expressing a sense of wonder that matched, indeed bettered, the sense of wonder I felt at that age (around ten) about everything I turned my mind to, including at the far reach such matters as light from extinguished stars still traveling toward us though their sources had been snuffed out. In effect, she was inviting me to extend *my* world of wonder to encompass *hers*. She was not just *informing* me. She was, rather, negotiating the world of wonder and possibility. Molecules, solids, liquids, movement were not facts; they were to be used in pondering and imagining. Miss Orcutt was the rarity. She was a human event, not a transmission device. It is not that my other teachers did not mark their stances. It was rather that their stances were so off-puttingly and barrenly informative. What was there to think about, even of Ethan Allen, except that he was what he was, a foxy mountain man. My chums and I fixed *our* stance to him all right: we incorporated him in our backyard play, created a Ticonderoga that had the school's beat a mile, and to this day I remember that battle on 10 May 1775! I was wounded, of course.

Each fact we encounter comes wrapped in stance marking. But now take the next step. Some stance markings are invitations to the use of thought, reflection, elaboration, fantasy. Let me put the matter in more formal terms. As John Searle puts it, it is the illocutionary force and not the locution that signifies the speaker's intent. And if the teacher wishes to close down the process of wondering by flat declarations of fixed factuality, he or she can do so. The teacher can also open wide a topic of locution to speculation and negotiation. To the extent that the materials of education are chosen for their amenableness to imaginative transformation and are presented in a light to invite negotiation and speculation, to that extent education becomes a part of what I earlier called "culture making." The pupil, in effect, becomes a party to the negotiatory process by which facts are created and interpreted. He becomes at once an agent of knowledge making as well as a recipient of knowledge transmission.

Let me digress for a moment. Some years ago I wrote some very insistent articles about the importance of discovery learning—learning on one's own, or as Piaget put it later (and I think better), learning by inventing. What I am proposing here is an extension of that idea, or better, a completion. My model of the child in those days was very much in the tradition of the solo child mastering the world by representing it to himself in his own terms. In the intervening years I have come increasingly to recognize that most learning in most settings is a communal activity, a sharing of the culture. It is not just that the child must make his knowledge his own, but that he must make it his own in a community of those who share his sense of belonging to a culture. It is this that leads me to emphasize not only discovery and invention but the importance of negotiating and sharing—in a word, of joint culture creating as an object of schooling and as an appropriate step en route to becoming a member of the adult society in which one lives out one's life.

❧

Much of the process of education consists of being able to distance oneself in some way from what one knows by being able to reflect on one's own knowledge. In most contemporary theories of cognitive development, this has been taken to mean the achievement of more abstract knowledge through Piagetian formal operations or by the use of more abstract symbolic systems. And it is doubtless true that in many spheres of knowledge, as in the sciences, one does indeed climb to "intellectually higher ground" (to use Vygotsky's phrase) by this route. One does indeed come to see arithmetic as a special case when one reaches the more abstract domain of algebra. But I think it is perilous to look at intellectual growth exclusively in this manner, for one will surely distort the meaning of intellectual maturity if one uses such a model exclusively.

It is not that I now "understand" *Othello* more abstractly than I did at fifteen when I first encountered that dark play. It is not even that I know more about pride, envy, and jealousy than I did then. Nor am I sure that I even understand better the furies that drove Iago to scheme the destruction of his boss and what kind of driven innocence kept the Moor from recognizing the destruction toward which his jealousy of Desdemona was leading him. Rather, it is that I have come to recognize in the play a theme, a plight, something nonadventitious about the human condition. I do not think that my interest in theater and literature has made me more *abstract*. Instead, it has joined me to the possible worlds that provide the landscape for thinking about the human condition, the human condition as it exists in the culture in which I live. But as I tried to say in Chapter 2, it is not simply the telling of tales, not the *fabula*, that produces reflection on plight in *Othello*, but the mode of discourse, the *sjuzet*. The play is not simply "about" a Moor trapped into jealousy of his wife by a hatefully scheming and envious, perhaps psychopathic, subordinate. Its language and craft as a play, the stances in which the playwright casts his characters, its dramatic speech act (in Iser's sense), makes the drama reverberate in our reflection. It is an invitation to reflection about manners, morals, and the human condition. This is not abstraction in the usual sense, but rather a sense of the complexities that can occur in narratives of human action.

But I do not for a minute believe that one can teach even mathematics or physics without transmitting a sense of stance toward nature and toward the use of mind. One cannot avoid committing oneself, given the nature of natural language, to a stance as to whether something is, say, a "fact" or the "consequence of a conjecture." The idea that any *humanistic* subject can be taught without revealing one's stance toward matters of human pith and substance is, of course, nonsense. It is equally true that if one does not choose, as a vehicle for teaching this form of "human distancing," something that touches the bone in some way or other (however one characterizes the psychological processes involved), one creates another nonsense. For what is needed is a basis for discussing not simply the content of what is before one, but the possible stances one might take toward it.

I think it follows from what I have said that the language of education, if it is to be an invitation to reflection and culture creating, cannot be the so-called uncontaminated language of fact and "objectivity." It must express stance and must invite counter-stance and in the process leave place for reflection, for metacognition. It is this that permits one to reach higher ground, this process of objectifying in language or image what one has thought and then turning around on it and reconsidering it.

❧

A few years ago when I was lecturing at the University of Texas, a group of students in the Honors School asked whether I would meet with them in one of their seminars. They wanted to discuss education. It was very lively indeed. Halfway through, a young woman said she wanted to ask me a question. She said she had just read my *Process of Education*, in which I had said that any subject could be taught to any child at any age in some form that was honest. I thought, "Here comes the question about calculus in the first grade." But not at all. No, her question was, "How do you know what's honest?" It stunned me. She had something in mind all right. Was I prepared to be honestly open in treating a child's ideas about a subject, was our *transaction* going to be honest? Was I going to be myself and let the child be himself or herself?

This brings me to my next topic. When we talk about the process of distancing oneself from one's thoughts, reflecting better to gain perspectives, does this not imply something about the knower? Are we not in some way talking about the forming of Self? It is a topic that makes me acutely uncomfortable. I have always tried to avoid concepts like Self, and where I have been forced to the wall, I have shinnied my way out by talking about "executive routines" and recursive loops and utterance-repair strategies. The discussion of the "transactional self" in Chapter 4 was an attempt to turn over a new leaf. For in some inescapable way, reflection implies a reflecting agent, metacognition requires a master routine that knows how and when to break away from straight processing to corrective processing procedures. Indeed, culture creating of the negotiatory kind I have been discussing involves an active participant. How shall we deal with Self?

I am by long persuasion (as the reader will know by now) a constructivist, and just as I believe that we construct or constitute the world, I believe too that Self is a construction, a result of action and symbolization. Like Clifford Geertz and Michelle Rosaldo, I think of Self as a text about how one is situated with respect to others and toward the world—a canonical text about powers and skills and dispositions that change as one's situation changes from young to old, from one kind of setting to another. The interpretation of this text *in situ* by an individual *is* his sense of self in that situation. It is composed of expectations, feelings of esteem and power, and so on. I have tried to make this point clear in my discussion of character in fiction in Chapter 2.

One of the most powerful ways of controlling and shaping participants in a society is through canonical images of selfhood of the kind presented in Chapter 2. It is accomplished in subtle ways—even to the nature of the toys we give children. Let me give you Roland Barthes's description of how French toys create *consumers* of French culture rather than *creators* of new cultural forms. Its wittiness, parenthetically, provides a classic instance of distancing.

> French toys: one could not find a better illustration of the fact that the adult Frenchman sees the child as another self. All the toys that one commonly sees are a microcosm of the adult world; they are all reduced copies of human objects . . .
>
> Invented forms are very rare: a few sets of blocks, which appeal to the spirit of do-it-yourself, are the only ones which offer dynamic forms. As for the others, French toys *always mean something,* and this something is always entirely socialized, constituted by the myths or techniques of adult life . . .
>
> The fact that the French *literally* prefigure the world of adult functions obviously cannot but prepare the child to accept them all, by constituting for him, even before he can think about it, the alibi of a Nature that has at all times created soldiers, postmen, and Vespas. Toys here reveal the list of things that the adult does not find at all unusual: war, bureaucracy, ugliness, Martians . . . French toys are like a Jivaro head, in which one

> recognizes, shrunk to the size of an apple, the wrinkles and hair of an adult . . . Faced with this world of faithful and complicated objects, the child can only identify himself as owner, as user, never as creator; he does not invent the world, he uses it; there are prepared for him actions without adventure, without wonder, without joy.

What Barthes might then have mentioned is that French culture becomes an aspect of French selfhood. Once furnished with its canonical images and formulae for reckoning, the young Frenchman or Frenchwoman becomes a seasoned operator of the system and a seasoned deployer of self. What better exemplification of the process than the production of writers like Barthes, masters of polished self-mockery?

The research of Michael Cole, Sylvia Scribner, and their colleagues on cross-cultural aspects of cognition illustrates the same general point in a more systematic way—the extent to which, for example, the indigenous mode of approaching knowledge is to take it from authority in contrast to a more Western European version of generating it oneself, autonomously, once one has acquired the constituents of reckoning from the society. As Cole and his colleagues point out, the introduction of a mode of schooling in which one "figures out things for oneself" changes one's conception of oneself and one's role, and also undermines the role of authority that exists generally within the culture, even to the point of being marked by modes of address reserved for those in authority.

If we relate this now to the issue to which we have been addressing ourselves—the conduct of schooling and the language in which it is carried out—we see that there is an immediate implication that follows from the "two-faced" nature of language, that it serves the double function of being both a mode of communication and a medium for representing the world about which it is communicating. *How* one *talks* comes eventually to be how one *represents* what one talks about. The stance and the negotiation over stance, by the same token, become features of the world toward which one is taking stances. And in time, as one develops a sense of one's self, the same pattern works its way into the manner in which we interpret that "text" which is our reading of ourselves. Just as Barthes's little Frenchman becomes a consumer and user of French modes of thinking and doing, so the little American comes to reflect the ways in which knowledge is gained and reflected upon in America, and the little American self comes to reflect the set of stances that in American culture one can actively (or passively) take toward knowledge.

If he fails to develop any sense of what I shall call reflective intervention in the knowledge he encounters, the young person will be operating continually from the outside in—knowledge will control and guide him. If he succeeds in developing such a sense, he will control and select knowledge as needed. If he develops a sense of self that is premised on his ability to penetrate knowledge for his own uses, and if he can share and negotiate the result of his penetrations, then he becomes a member of the culture-creating community.

❧

Earlier in this chapter I mentioned two lines of inquiry that shed some light on the processes I have been discussing. One was that of Vygotsky, about whom I commented in Chapter 5; the other is contained in a volume by Hugh Mehan called *Learning Lessons*. To Vygotsky we owe a special debt for elucidating some of the major relations between language, thought, and socialization. His basic view, recall, was that conceptual learning was a collaborative enterprise involving an adult who enters into dialogue with the child in a fashion that provides the child with hints and props that allow him to begin a new climb, guiding the child in next steps before the child is capable of appreciating their significance on his own. It is the "loan of consciousness" that gets the child through the zone of proximal development. The model is Socrates guiding the slave boy through geometry in the *Meno*. It is a procedure, by the way, that works as well in Elkton, Virginia, as in classical Athens, as we know from the promising research of Alan Collins and his colleagues on Socratic tutoring programs.

Mehan's work illustrates the extent to which the process of exchange and negotiation—this culture creating—is a feature of classroom routines and procedures. It is not simply that the individual learner works his solo way through the lesson, but that the lesson itself is an exercise in collectivity, one that depends upon the attunement of the teacher to the expressions and intents of members of a class.

I can sum up the message this way. Language not only transmits, it creates or constitutes knowledge or "reality." Part of that reality is the stance that the language implies toward knowledge and reflection, and the generalized set of stances one negotiates creates in time a sense of one's self. Reflection and "distancing" are crucial aspects of achieving a sense of the range of possible stances—a metacognitive step of huge import. The language of education is the language of culture creating, not of knowledge consuming or knowledge acquisition alone. In a time when our educational establishment has produced alienation from the process of education, nothing could be more practical than to look afresh in the light of modern ideas in linguistics and the philosophy of language at the consequences of our present school talk and at its possible transformations.

10

Developmental Theory as Culture

Let me begin with what should by now seem a reasonable proposition. Theories of human development, once accepted into the prevailing culture, no longer operate simply as descriptions of human nature and its growth. By their nature, as accepted cultural representations, they, rather, give a social reality to the processes they seek to explicate and, to a degree, to the "facts" that they adduce in their support. It is much as a theory of property is constitutive of concepts like ownership, trespass, and inheritance. By so endowing them with *social* reality, we give them a practical embodiment as well. So there is not only "real property" but real estate agents, mortgage companies, and even protest novels like *The Grapes of Wrath*.

Theories of development, by their stipulations about human growth, also create rules and institutions that are just as compelling as mortgage companies: delinquency, truancy, "milestones of growth," national standards. Elections to the local school board are determined by whether the children of the community are achieving above or below national norms for reading. Norms, of course, are dependent on the theory of reading that is by now implicitly embodied in the institutionalized culture of school. In an even more emotionally beset domain, theory determines what we take to be the normal growth of sexuality in children. Though we are curiously insensitive about such an obvious point in our own culture, we accept it when we encounter it in the pages of Mead's *Coming of Age in Samoa* or of Malinowski's *Sexual Life of Savages*.

All of which is not to say that students of human development do not subject their ideas and hypotheses to empirical test in the usual way of scientists. Rather, it is in the nature of things that, once "findings" are accepted into the implicit knowledge that constitutes culture, once-scientific theories become as reality defining, prescriptive, and canonical as the folk-psychological theories they replaced.

Someone will object that a "tested" theory is *true,* while a folk theory is some compound of human wishes, fears, and habits. The distinction is important. But truth is better understood in Nelson Goodman's sense—as "rightness." The truth of theories of light—wave or corpuscular—is "true" only for particular contexts. That is their rightness. By the same token, the truths of theories of development are relative to the cultural contexts in which they are applied. But that relativity is not, as in physics, a question of logical consistency alone. Here it is also a question of congruence with values that prevail in the culture. It is this congruence that gives developmental theories—proposed initially as mere descriptions—a moral face once they have become embodied in the broader culture.

Human culture, of course, is one of the two ways by which "instructions" about how humans should grow are carried from one generation to the next—the other being the human genome. The plasticity of the human genome is such that there is no unique way in which it is realized, no way that is independent of opportunities provided by the culture into which an individual is born. Recall Sir Peter Medawar's *bon mot* about nature and nurture: each contributes 100 percent to the variance of the phenotype. Man is not free of *either* his genome *or* his culture. Human culture simply provides *ways* of development among the many that are made possible by our plastic genetic inheritance. Those ways are prescriptions about the canonical course of human growth. To say, then, that a theory of development is "culture free" is to make not a wrong claim, but an absurd one.

It is inevitable, then, that theories of human development are "sciences of the artificial" (in Herbert Simon's sense), however much they may also be descriptive of "nature." As such, they may with profit be examined in the same spirit in which an anthropologist studies, say, theories of ethnobotany or ethnomedicine to deepen his understanding of a culture in general or, for that matter, to deepen his understanding of a culture's way of dealing with nutrition or disease. It does not denigrate a theory of human development to study it in this way. The economist, to take a parallel case, would certainly not take offense if one sought to study, say, how such "realities" as money supply, measured by M1 or M2, affect the conduct of banking or equity trading, nor would he cringe at the charge that both measures *are* realities to which banking and market trading react. It is vacuous to reply that money supply "existed" before the measures of them were known and available—just as vacuous as to say that repression "existed" before our attention was drawn to it by psychoanalysis.

What I shall do in the following pages is to explore how the three modern titans of developmental theory—Freud, Piaget, and Vygotsky—may be constituting the realities of growth in our culture rather than merely describing them. I should also have access to "informants" in the culture much as an anthropologist would in a field study. That would permit me to do the anthropology properly: to map popular beliefs and relate them to the corpus of each theory, tracing the transformations that have occurred. I do not. Rather, I shall operate in the more intuitive spirit of an intellectual historian, and even then with a glaring deficiency. For I am writing in advance of history. At the end, I shall look back as best I can and try to estimate how the three titans may be viewed in the future.

Let me begin, by way of illustration and "warmup," with brief accounts of how two older theories of mind changed common sense about the nature and "reality" of mind. Two distinguished historians provide material: Crane Brinton, whose *Anatomy of Revolution* includes an evaluation of the cultural impact of John Locke, Montesquieu, and Voltaire on the American Revolution; and J. B. Bury, in whose classic, *The Idea of Progress,* the impact of an idea about the uses of mind is explored historically.

Brinton notes that Locke's power in the New World was to elevate nature to the role of supreme arbiter in human affairs—elevate it to the point where invoking it came naturally to intellectuals, pamphleteers, and eventually ordinary people. Iniquitous acts—"Ship Money in England, Stamp Act in America, patents of nobility in France, were all contrary to the law of nature."

For Locke's appeal was in proposing implicitly that Everyman could learn directly from nature—from his own experience of it, without the intervention of higher authority. At a stroke, Divine Rights and Divine Revelation were disposed of with scarcely a word about either, except that both ran counter to nature. By arguing that nothing is in the mind save what gets there through the senses, Locke created a base in common sense for a democracy of experience and thought. And while Boston (especially Harvard) did not take kindly to sedition against the crown or to Sam Adams's pamphlets, it was prepared to grant that the New World was a different world (nature again) and that the new "American" understood it as those at a distance could not. Empiricism, the appeal to nature as knowable by the common man, was a powerful, if implicit, premise of the American Revolution.

To be sure, Locke did not *invent* empiricism: it had flourished before him in Hobbes and grew afterwards in the writings of Bishop Berkeley and David Hume. Note that all four of them lived in a period of rising mercantilism when prospering merchants were seeking an equal footing with king and church, or at least freedom from exploitation. It is not simply that philosophers of mind do or do not resonate with the spirit of the times. Rather, it is that the times were ready to convert premises of technical philosophy into canons of popular culture.

Locke had a cultural "impact" in the small and in the large. Thoughtful men like Jefferson weighed the consequences of his doctrines in thinking of the shape of a state. The Bill of Rights to the Constitution, formulated at Philadelphia a century after Locke, was an embodiment of his technical ideas translated into institutional terms. And in the small, the Charter of Germantown Friends School in that very city was an embodiment of those same ideas filtered through the pragmatic mind of Benjamin Franklin. Pupils were to be sensitized to the riches of experience, better to create a democracy of knowledge.

The idea of progress has no comparable parentage—though Bury gives pride of parentage to Francis Bacon. Bury sees its emergence as a liberation from older conceptions of Fate, entrenched conceptions stemming from the classical Greek myth of the decline of man from the Golden Age of the Gods to the Age of Brass. Fate was sealed; human effort could delay but could not prevent it. Christianity, after it, promised little more on earth for proper human effort, only entry into the kingdom of heaven afterwards. Practical effort, indeed, put one at risk, in Christian theology, of not making it through the eye of a needle.

Bury sees Bacon's *Novum Organum* as the turning point. Man, on Bacon's view, could by his own efforts penetrate the truths of nature and act upon those truths in his own behalf. By doing so, he could assure a continuity of progress, almost an inevitability. Progress was contingent upon the exercise of mind.

And so Jonathan Edwards (Perry Miller tells us) could preach to his frontier parishioners in Northampton, Massachusetts, less than a century later, having just read in a newly received *Proceedings* of the Royal Society about Newton's demonstration that white light was composed of a spectral mix, that man had unlocked yet another of God's secrets and could aspire to further success in doing so, to the glory of both God and man. Again, impact in the large as in the small. The Royal Society and the Massachusetts Institute of Technology, three centuries removed in their founding, were both premised on the idea of progress. And indeed, nearly four centuries later, a distinguished graduate of the latter institution, a close friend of mine, admitted to me while we lunched together in the garden of a seventeenth-century Irish pub that this day was the tenth anniversary of his loss of faith in the idea of progress! He is a man I know well and respect greatly. I knew him in the decade before his admitted loss of faith, as I had in the decade after. I can report that (at least from the outside) his loss had affected neither the conduct of his intellectual life nor the way in which he ran the research company of which he was head. Perhaps once a culture has become gripped by an idea of mind, its uses, and their consequences, it is impossible to shed the idea, even when one has lost faith in it.

For the impact of ideas about mind does not stem from their truth, but seemingly from the power they exert as possibilities embodied in the practices of a culture. Can you shed the concept of crime when there are courts, police, and prisons? And perhaps in the minds of men as well, possibility when widely enough accepted is translated into necessity. If it is held widely enough to be possible that man *can* learn from experience, then we arrange our conduct and our institutions in such a way that it is *necessary* that he learn from experience. We arrange tests to find whether he has, "remediate" him when he has not, and distribute subsequent opportunities accordingly. It is not a long walk from Germantown Friends to the Scholastic Achievement Test. Nor from the *Novum Organum* to meritocracy.

❧

Now our three titans: Freud, Vygotsky, and Piaget. Let me sketch briefly what seems to me to be the brunt of each theory—or rather, what I think will be the impact of each on commonsense conceptions of human growth, how each defines a viable cultural reality.

Freud's view, as cultural drama, is principally preoccupied with the past and with the means whereby man frees himself from the shackles of his own history. Though he disdained the role, Freud was in the great reform tradition. His metaphors—compounded of the language of hydraulics, of economics, and of rational moralism—were drenched in the imagery of reform: man, with the help of analysis, reforming himself. "Where there was Id, now there shall be Ego." His explications of the anatomy of unreason were framed in the idiom of undoing it. The hydraulic model of instincts pressing for release, the economic model of symptom formation in which neurosis is a bargain struck between the competing demands of conflicting impulses, and even the notion of the analytic situation as providing a microcosm (the transference neurosis) in which the larger neurosis could be explored under shelter—all of these were dedicated to exposing and undoing the fate into which one's history had cast one. Indeed, the very idea of the transference neurosis permitted the past to be projected into the present, so that it could be understood and exorcized through "working through." If at times he was a gloomy reformer, as in his post-World War *Future of an Illusion*, where the Death Instinct and the repetition compulsion are given a new role, he remained for all that a believer in man's capacity to achieve freedom from his past through psychoanalytically informed reason. As Louis Breger puts it, he was "essentially masculine, committed to objectivity and reason."

For all the resistance to Freud and his doctrines—particularly to the idea of infant sexuality and to what was seen as his "sexual reductionism"—he was greeted then and continues to be greeted by literary intellectuals now as a liberator. His impact on the novel, on drama, and even on the writing of history has far exceeded his impact on the human sciences. For while the human sciences have turned increasingly to a sociopolitical structural interpretation of man's fate, in which, say, capitalism rather than the unconscious is the *fons et origo* of psychic suffering, the literary intellectual finds in Freud the new model of the human tragedy, even the sources of its humor. The "hero" is not so much he who succeeds in the struggle against the dark forces created by his history, but he who is aware. The hero becomes an Epistemic Epitome who, if he does not triumph in the coarse precincts of action, triumphs at least in psychic reality. He understands.

I am indebted to Richard Rorty for an insight into Freud's formulation of Unreason as embodied in the Id, and it sheds light on the issue at hand. Unreason, before Freud, had been depicted as a blind brute, enraged and stupid. Freud was the first to cast it (as Milton had cast Satan in *Paradise Lost*, and C. S. Lewis in *The Screwtape Letters*) in the role of a principled and clever opponent. Unreason is a creator of wit, an artificer of slips of the tongue, a hard bargainer in the transactions of ego defense. To be sure, the Ego must learn to control the charging horse that is Id (to take one of Freud's metaphors), but he had better be a clever rider if he hopes to succeed at it—not just because the horse is a strong plunger, but also because he is full of guile.

So "the shrink" becomes both friend and tutelary battleground for Everyman—friend in the sense of advocate, and a "battlefield simulation" whereon the old wars can be successfully reenacted this time around. So rooted has this image become both in psychoanalytic theory and in the literary imagination that there is the liveliest resistance to any reformulation that reduces the role of the past and diminishes the importance of the struggle against it. Contemporary proposals, for example, that urge an abandonment of the "archaeological premise" in Freud—the importance of finding and rooting out *past* trauma—are greeted with hostility. It is not enough that one create a rich and generative narrative of one's life without locating when, where, and how the traumas occurred, even if they were only imagined at the time.

If Freud was the architect of a new and rich edifice of the past and a prescriber of recipes for altering its impact, Piaget's theory advocates the self-sufficiency of the present as an explanation of itself. The explanation of children's thought can be found *within* the intrinsic logic of particular stages of development—not in the past history of the child. Mental operations are governed by a logic in force in the present, and as the logic changes from stage to stage in development, that does not give the past control of the present, but the present control of the past.

Old ways of thinking are encompassed as special cases in new ways of thinking. Whatever happens by way of "history" is *aliment* (literally pablum) to the growth of thought. Thought digests this aliment in a fashion compatible with its present internal logic.

There is neither reform nor liberation in the Piagetian canon, and it would be absurd to imagine a protest movement against, say, the sway of concrete operations. With aliment appropriate to a particular stage, it will be converted to the next stage. Should the pupa rage about not yet being a butterfly?

If for Freud the key lay in the informed struggle against the past, for Piaget it was in the appropriate nourishment of the present. For him, the drama was the child's reinvention of the world, a constant and recurring process achieved through action on the world in the present that, with time, transformed the child's previous logic into a new logical *structure d'ensemble* that (as noted) included the old as a special case. Freud looked to drama, literature, and myth for his metaphors of historical plight. Piaget turned to the logician and the epistemologist for his account of how logical structures are formed and then transformed.

For Piaget, growth happened naturally. To ask how one can hasten it was to ask "la question americaine." The drama consisted in honoring its natural growth, not in comparing its present status with what it would later be or might become under some special curricular dispensation. It is this respectful explication of the self-sufficiency and dignity of the child's mind *in terms of its own logic* that is now finding its way into the canonical forms of the culture. It has begun to have a profound effect on commonsense education. Piaget's motto, "To learn is to invent," may yet alter the view that to teach is simply to transmit, to fill a vacuum.

Of Vygotsky we need consider little beyond what has already been said in Chapter 5. For him, the mind grows neither naturally nor unassisted. It is determined neither by its history nor by the logical constraints of its present operations. Intelligence, for him, is readiness to use culturally transmitted knowledge and procedures as prostheses of mind. But much depends upon the availability and the distribution of those prosthetic devices within a culture. Vygotsky is a growth theorist whose ideas could serve liberation ideology far better than the romanticisms of a Paolo Freire or an Ivan Illitch. At the same time, his is a view of the nurturing of mind that fits, say, the Oxford tutorial system or the discussion methods of the elite academy far better than it fits the ordinary common school—whether in America, Cuba, or Russia. It gives heart to liberation ideologies by its concentration on the importance of a *social* support system for leading the child through the famous zone of proximal development. But it actually describes the method of the well-conceived tutorial or small discussion group.

Stephen Toulmin described Vygotsky as the Mozart of psychology, which surely captures his genius, his early prodigiousness, and his death. Unlike Mozart, he was not widely appreciated in his time. But if ever there is to be an age in which we cease thinking of the growth of mind as a lonely voyage of each on his own, one in which culture (in its old pejorative sense of "high culture") is valued not only for its treasures but for its tool kit of procedures for achieving higher ground, then Vygotsky will be rediscovered. The irony, of course, is that his avowed impulse was Marxist. His ideas are in jeopardy again in the Soviet Union; they have never had a broad following elsewhere, though it begins to increase as his works are translated. He is certainly no Mozart where listeners are concerned! He is indeed a Sleeping Giant—perhaps as Carnot was for thermodynamics, unassimilated until the time came ripe, and then made a Founding Father.

The "cultural posture" of a theory of development is sometimes reflected in the place it assigns language in the growth process. I do not mean to make an obscure point. By a cultural posture I mean only the manner in which the theory relates the growing individual to the culture at large, since language is the coin in which that relationship is effected. The same claim could probably be made about the place of education in a theory of development (a point I made in passing in the preceding chapter). The role of language, however, is particularly interesting since it implies a view as well about the symbolic environment and how one is presumed to operate within it. Just as an example, it may well have been Pavlov's recognition that a stimulus-substitution theory of conditioning could not cope with the impact of ideological revolution that led him to formulate the Second Signal System (discussed in Chapter 5). Though he held himself aloof from Soviet ideology, he obviously could not remain completely above the revolution that was going on about him. There is no evidence that the Second Signal System was a "lackey" reaction on Pavlov's part—indeed the Soviet authorities were courting him as a distinguished Nobel Laureate they were glad to have in their midst. Yet, seeing the changes that were being triggered by ideological doctrine (as well as by armed force), he must have sensed the limitation of his earlier views. Obviously this is a conjecture, but it leads me to look again at our three titans in a similar spirit.

We know already that Vygotsky adopted as one of his central metaphors the notion of two separate streams of development that flowed together: a stream of thought and a stream of language. Inner speech was for him a regulatory process that, in Dewey's famous words, provided a means for sorting one's thoughts about the world. And in a somewhat Deweyesque fashion, he also saw language as embodying cultural history. It was not surprising then that language could provide the way to "higher ground"—culturally as well as in abstract conceptual terms. And, of course, the "voyage across the Zone" through the tutorial process was made possible only by language.

Yet language served a much more progressive role for Vygotsky than being simply a vehicle for the transmission of cultural history. He was acquainted, as I noted in Chapter 5, with the Russian literary-linguistic tradition, from Baudouin de Courtenay through Jakobson and Bakhtin, in which the *generativeness* of language played such a central role not only in the contemporary sense of that term but also in the sense of being a "raiser of consciousness." What could bespeak his concerns more clearly than the title of his major work: *Thought and Language*. For Vygotsky, language was an agent for altering the powers of thought—giving thought new means for explicating the world. In turn, language became the repository for new thoughts once achieved.

Freud, of course, formulated a theory that gave a new base to the old idea of the "talking cure." Language was for him a battleground on which warring impulses fought for their claims. If Freud were remembered only for his daring interpretation of "slips of the tongue," he would still go down in history as a great innovator. But, curiously, he gave little attention to language as such—to its generative powers, its powers of control, its role as a repository of cultural history. True to his archaeological conviction in the importance of finding and exposing the remains of the early and archaic in the psyche, he turned his attention to the metaphoric in the conviction that this was the mode in which dreams and the unconscious spoke. The "instruction" that the patient receives at the start of his analysis is to "say whatever comes to mind," that by so doing, his troubled and repressed past will find expression. Dreams, too were conceived as a language, which if read correctly revealed the patient's hidden agenda. So Freud's interest in language, for all his own sensitivities as a gifted writer and reader, was principally in its power to express the archaic and the repressed. Would he have approved of Lacan's "semiotization" of psychoanalysis? Probably not.

It is a pity that the inwardness of Freud's circle, so evident in Ernest Jones's biography, kept Freud so isolated from the philosophical debates of his Vienna. At very least he would have had antagonists on whom to sharpen his wits. For the Vienna Circle was in those years ruling out of philosophy all statements not subject to empirical or analytic verifiability: they were "nonsense," though as John Austin ruefully remarked they constituted three-quarters of what ordinary human beings said. Freud, of course, was arguing that such "nonsense" was what told us about human intentions and about the human condition. He might even have come to know more of an ex-Viennese, then removed to Cambridge: Ludwig Wittgenstein. Wittgenstein, not unlike Freud, saw the philosopher as "helping the fly out of the bottle." He conceived of language as expressing "language games," and these in turn expressed "forms of life," each to be understood in its own terms. Freud too, I think, saw language, whether spoken by patients on the couch or by the man in the street, as an expression of an inner life that had stabilized into neurosis or character. No surprise, then, that for him talk was both the vehicle for diagnosis and the medium for cure.

For Piaget, language *reflects* thought and does not determine it in any sense. That the internal logic of thought is expressed in language has no effect on the logic itself. The logic of concrete operations or of later formal operations is what keeps thought on the track, and these two logical systems are *structures d'ensemble* on their own, unaffected by the language in which they are expressed. In Piaget and Inhelder's book on the logic of the adolescent, they remark that ancient cultures may not have had formal operations. But the remark is more in the spirit of discussing scientific progress (which Piaget saw as paralleling the course of the child's growth) than in appreciation of the enabling role of a culture's symbolic tool kit. If one already *had* formal operations—the capacity to operate directly on symbols rather than on what they refer to in the world—then and only then would a culture's stored knowledge be accessible. But at that, the stored knowledge and the notational system in which it was couched would not affect the nature of the thought processes of those who used them. Those were inherent, nurtured to their own form of maturity by the aliment of experience gained in action, not in talk.

Each view, then, expresses a cultural posture. Freud's expresses his "liberationism" through a strategy of outsmarting conventional language by "free" association. Piaget's expresses his faith in the inherent logic of thought and subordinates language to it. Vygotsky's gives language both a cultural past and a generative present, and assigns it a role as the nurse and tutor of thought. Freud faces the present from the past: growth is by freeing. Piaget respects the inviolate integrity of the present: growth is the nurturing of intrinsic logic. And Vygotsky turns the cultural past into the generative present by which we reach toward the future: growth is reaching.

❧

Miracle that we should have had three such titans in a generation, and good fortune they were that divergent. If all three should succeed in recreating the culture, it will be the richer for their diversity, however discordant that diversity may become.

Yet, in spite of their greatness, each of our titans has come in for renewed attack; each is open to new criticism in the perspective of the changed culture that they helped to create. None of them can be said to have "settled into" the culture. Indeed, the contemporary attacks on all three of them might even be interpreted as a sign of their vigor, although it is now the vigor of the past rather than of the future. For it must surely be the case that effective innovators succeed not only by reshaping culture by their primary contribution, but by forcing a shape on the criticisms that eventually dislodge them. In Nelson Goodman's terms, once we take their once fresh innovations as our givens and then go beyond them, what remains behind is not them, but their effects "in the guts of the living." I think we can already see this "digestive" process at work, and I would like to end this essay with a speculative diagnosis of how the impact of Freud, of Vygotsky, and of Piaget will fare in the future.

Take Freud first. He is already seen by many critics as a victim of the historicism that shaped his imagination. As in Amélie Rorty's account of the personae of literature (see Chapter 2), his world is peopled with *figures:* "their roles and their traits emerge from their place in an ancient narrative"—narratives of family and the plights it creates for the child. Donald Spence (whose book bears the revealing title *Narrative Truth and Historical Truth*) attacks Freud for his "archaeological premise": that therapy is accomplished through discovery of the traumas of one's past. Spence argues, instead, that what matters is that therapy permit the reconstruction of a life in the form of a narrative of the whole, and that a detailed archaeological reconstruction is in itself not the crucial matter. From another side comes the criticism that Freud's *figures* (again in Rorty's sense) are without sufficient selfhood. The revisions of Hans Kohut demand a place for considering how self develops, not simply how figures in the family plot manage to form their ego defenses. And in a related vein, Roy Schafer, seeking to reformulate the language of psychoanalysis, asks that patients use a language of action that includes within its scope a concept of responsibility for how one acts—again, in Rorty's terms, a move toward "selfhood." And in a perceptive essay, Henri Zukier complains that there is no concept of development in Freud save the repetition compulsion. In consequence, narrative-bound figures emerge, not individuals.

All of which does not diminish Freud or belittle his enormous influence. Rather, the criticisms speak to contemporary concerns that in some interesting way could not exist but for the sensibility that Freud's original formulations helped bring into existence. Freud's version of man's plight was a "right version" of a possible world for his time and place. A great part of the new sensibility depended for its growth upon the destruction of earlier forms of reticence—not only about sexuality, but also about subjectivity in general. It was that sensibility that helped create not only the writers—the Joyces, Gides, Becketts, Lawrences, Bellows—but also the readers whose virtual texts could be shaped by the novels they were reading. In the end, it was this new sensibility that rejected the classical Freudian image.

Or take Piaget. It is not unfair to say that he falls with structuralism—despite the powerful influence his structuralist views have had on our conception of the child's mind and, indeed, of mind in general. But again, structuralism brought about the sensibility that destroyed *it*. In linguistics, where it was born, it had an astonishingly illuminating effect—as in Saussure's insistence upon the semiotic interdependence of all elements of language within the system of language as a whole. But transposed to the human condition in the broad, it had glaring deficiencies, deficiencies that could not be suspected until the very idea of structure was applied. There was no place for use and intention, only for an analysis of the products of mind taken in the abstract. So there was no place for human dilemmas, for tragic plights, for local knowledge encapsulated in bias. Piaget's very *program,* his "genetic epistemology," was insufficiently human: to trace the history of mathematics and science in the growth of the child's mind. But what light does that shed on the history of sensibility, of "madness," of alienation, or of passions? If Freud was *au fond* a moralist, as Philip Rieff argues so eloquently, was Piaget enough of a one? Can we understand the uneven bursts of moral passion or the rise of guile in human growth from his account of moral development? Even from within the Piagetian fold, the research of Kohlberg, Colby, and others points to the raggedness and irregularity of the so-called stages of moral development. Particularity, localness, context, historical opportunity, all play so large a role that it is embarrassing to have them outside Piaget's system rather than within. But they cannot fit within. Any more than "local expertise" with no overspill into "general intelligence" can be fitted into the Piagetian system of the stages of intellectual development. So in the system of moral development, there is no means of tracing the emergence of a Coriolanus, an Iago, a Lord Jim, any more than there is of tracing the emergence of an Einstein, a Bohr, or (in spite of Howard Gruber's fine book) of a Darwin. More modestly, the system failed to capture the particularity of Everyman's knowledge, the role of negotiations in establishing meaning, the tinkerer's way of encapsulating knowledge rather than generalizing it, the muddle of ordinary moral judgment. As a system, it (like Freud's) failed to yield a picture of self and of individuality. Yet, for all that, Piaget's accomplishments were gigantic. Deconstruction, well executed, elucidates the structures that it modifies by analysis, even if in the end it replaces them. In the end, thanks to Piaget, we shall have a better sense of what self, what individuality, what local knowledge mean.

Of Vygotsky, we can sense already (though his impetus is far from spent) the kind of criticism that is rising. "It smacks so of twentieth-century liberalism," a literary critic friend said to me after I had put him on to Vygotsky. Is the Zone of Proximal Development always a blessing? May it not be the source of human vulnerability to persuasion, vulnerability because the learner begins without a proper basis for criticizing what is being "fed" to him by ones whose consciousness initially exceeds his own? Is higher ground better ground? *Whose* higher ground? And are those sociohistorical forces that shape the language that then shapes the minds of those who use it, are those forces always benign? The language, after all, is being reshaped by massive corporations, by police states, by those who would create an efficient European market or an invincible America living under a shield of lasers. Indeed, was not Vygotsky's famous example of conceptual development illustrated by how the mind improves when armed with the Marxist ideas of state? Yet, rather ironically in this case, it is Vygotsky's systematic analysis that, in the end, makes us most keenly aware of the dangers to which the critics of the future will address themselves.

But to say this much about Freud, Piaget, and Vygotsky and of the future of their impact is to say not quite enough. For I have not said anything about what seems to me to be at the heart of contemporary sensibility beyond what was put there by the insights of our three titans. We are living through a cultural revolution that shapes our image of the future in a way that nobody, however titanic, could have foreseen a half-century ago. It is a revolution whose shape we cannot sense, although we already sense its depth. We are in danger of annihilating ourselves with unthinkably powerful weapons, and we cannot bear to think about it directly, for there is nothing we seem able to do to control the danger. We are, in consequence, in deep malaise, a malaise of futurelessness. It is difficult for any theory of human development to gain a hold on the "cultural imagination" of those who dread that there may be no future. For a theory of development is, *par excellence*, a future topic.

Under such circumstances, what can we expect to emerge by way of a theory of development that will be compelling enough to shape a new reality? For the time being, we will have modest theories, local in concern, free of grand concepts of future possibility: how to go from novice to expert in this domain, how to master that subject or that dilemma. These are the "domain specific" theories that are on the scene today. They have the virtue of fulfilling the daily needs of technical societies, providing "routine" futures. But I think this is a transition stage.

When and if we pass beyond the unspoken despair in which we are now living, when we feel we are again able to control the race to destruction, a new breed of developmental theory is likely to arise. It will be motivated by the question of how to create a new generation that can prevent the world from dissolving into chaos and destroying itself. I think that its central technical concern will be how to create in the young an appreciation of the fact that many worlds are possible, that meaning and reality are created and not discovered, that negotiation is the art of constructing new meanings by which individuals can regulate their relations with each other. It will not, I think, be an image of human development that locates all of the sources of change inside the individual, the solo child. For if we have learned anything from the dark passage in history through which we are now moving it is that man, surely, is not "an island, entire of itself" but a part of the culture that he inherits and then recreates. The power to recreate reality, to reinvent culture, we will come to recognize, is where a theory of development must begin its discussion of mind.

Afterword

After the manuscript of this book had been completed and sent off to the publisher, two original and thought provoking articles appeared in the *Times Literary Supplement* that, it seemed to me, required the courtesy of an Afterword. Each sketches a landscape of the literary-intellectual scene that demands either that one locate oneself in it or that, instead, one offer an alternative landscape. Both are concerned, in kindred ways (as I shall try to show), with a compelling moral issue: the worth and function of works of literary art and the criteria by which one judges (or denies that one *can* judge) their value. Since much of this book, often more implicitly than explicitly, is concerned with just such issues (particularly Chapters 1, 2, 3, and 7), it would be irresponsible for me to remain silent. For I have argued very hard for the view that a work of art does indeed serve a function, a morally justifiable and even essential function, and that its value as a work of art can be appreciated even if it cannot be measured.

The articles are by two very different literary critics: George Steiner and Tzvetan Todorov. Both Steiner's "A New Meaning of Meaning" (in the *TLS* of 8 November 1985 and taken from his 1985 Leslie Stephen Lecture at Cambridge) and Todorov's "All Against Humanity" (in the *TLS* of 4 October 1985 in the form of an essay review of Robert Scholes's book *Textual Power*) are explicit attacks on deconstruction in both spirit and method and, at the same time, implicit attacks on antihumanism both in modern literary scholarship and, at one step removed, in psychology. To do justice to them, as well as to represent the landscapes they sketch, I shall summarize each of their arguments separately with a view to casting them stereoscopically into a single image afterward.

Steiner begins with the seeming arbitrariness of all value judgments, aesthetic and moral alike: *de gustibus non disputandum,* "No aesthetic proposition can be termed either 'right' or 'wrong.' " On this view, the two principal "motions of spirit" in reading, interpretation and evaluation, cannot be separated, for to interpret is to judge. Yet, common sense tells us it is otherwise. There is an evident distinction between critical evaluation on the one side and interpretation on the other. The first is synchronic: "Aristotle's Oedipus is not negated or made obsolete by Hölderlin's; Hölderlin's is neither improved nor cancelled out by Freud's." But at the end of the road in the *interpretation* of a text, there *is* a "best" reading or a best set of readings that conform with philology or with biographical information about the writer's intent or with Flacius's principle, *historia est fundamentum scriptorae.* But, Steiner notes, it is precisely this "commonsense" assertion that is put at issue by post-structuralist deconstruction. What is the search for auctorial intention but an infinite regress? Do not trust the teller but the tale. Or better, why trust either? Why should a critical reading be secondary in status to the work of art that it criticizes? Let there be a democracy of all texts, an encompassing intertextuality—Steiner sums up the position this way: "language is simply being used about language in an infinitely self-multiplying series (the mirror arcade)." As for the commonsense assertion, the deconstructionist critic replies: What is common sense but a linguistic convention, a straw poll, a defensive posture of the academy?

And yet, "Across the millennia, a decisive majority of informed receivers has not only arrived at a manifold but broadly coherent view of what the *Iliad,* or *King Lear* or *The Marriage of Figaro,* is about (the meanings of their meaning), but have concurred in judging Homer, Shakespeare and Mozart to be supreme artists . . ." But Steiner is not satisfied with such a pragmatic response to so radical a challenge as deconstruction. "If counter-moves are worth exploring, they will be of an order no less radical than are those of the anarchic and even 'terrorist' grammatologists and masters of mirrors." The radical instrument is "moral intuition," whose most concentrated agencies are tact, courtesy of heart, the inwardly ethical, good taste. What is morally self-evident in this moral dispensation is that "the poem comes before the commentary," that (in Aristotle's sense) the poem is of the essence, commentary only an "accident" contingent on the essence. "The poem *is;* the commentary *signifies.*" To accept such a notion, Steiner argues, requires that we embrace a principle of transcendence.

It is a modest enough, rather Cartesian principle of transcendence. The transcendent is an unshakable, axiomatic acceptance of "meaning-fulness," like Descartes's axiom that God will not falsify our perceptions of the world or Einstein's that He will not play dice with us. It is a belief that meaning (or meanings) lies in the work of art, embodied, incarnate, a real presence—as truly sacramental as the faith, say, of a Rashi or a Nicholas of Lyra that the word of God could always and inevitably be found in the literal text of Scripture once it were properly explicated philologically, historically, and with a view to its function as theology. It is faith in meaning incarnate in the work of art, meaning that captures the "immensity of the commonplace," that changes our very construction of reality: "poplars are on fire after Van Gogh." So Matisse could proclaim after completing the murals in Vence, "I am God," or Picasso speak of "God, the other craftsman."

The literary artist, it would follow from this argument, becomes an agent in the evolution of mind—but not without the co-optation of the reader as his fellow author. Together they rediscover the "immensity of the commonplace" or, in Joyce's more reverent phrase, "epiphanies of the ordinary." By this token, there are not only great art and great artists, but great readers. It is a point to which Steiner's argument should lead him, though he does not make it explicitly (at least not in the *TLS* version). That is to say, once the leap of faith is taken, once one "accepts" the meaning-fulness of the work of art, there is still the task of personal transmutation: making the meaning in the text one's *own* meaning as a reader. This is the deep psychological problem: how the meaning "in" the text becomes a meaning "in" the head of a reader. And it is not resolved by invoking an act of faith.

In a way, resolution of the problem by appeal to faith in meaning-fulness is reminiscent of Luther's division of the universe into the kingdom of heaven and the kingdom of earth, faith being the instrument of the former, reason of the latter. You could not reason your way into belief in God's forgiveness: that must come by faith alone. But once the act of faith had, so to speak, been committed, it could be supported and enriched by "regenerate reason" operating in support of faith. I take Steiner to be saying that only after one has made a moral commitment to the possibility of transcendent meaning being incarnate in a work of art is it possible to "receive" that meaning with tact and taste and to apply to it the instruments of reason—regenerate reason in Luther's sense.

If I have caught the spirit of Steiner's account, it leaves two questions not so much unanswered but unasked. The first is about faith or belief in "meaning-fulness": why he thinks it is so fragile that it needs to be shored up by renewed acts of transcendence. The second is why he is so deeply disturbed about the power of deconstruction to destroy literary and moral values. I think these two may turn out to be variants of the same question.

Let me take the second question first. I suspect that Steiner is more concerned with the literary politics of deconstruction than with the doctrine itself—a point to which I will return in discussing Todorov. For surely there have been radical "perspectivalists" at large since at least the time of the Ockhamists—clever men asking whether meaning (and the reality to which it presumed to make reference) was in the world or in the word. There were by no means all "masters of mirrors"—though some of them were. Nor is it unusual for there to be battles over what theologians call "canonicity": which text to accept as primary and which as secondary; which, so to speak, is the real thing and which a commentary on it. Indeed, the presence of radical perspectivalism often had the good effect of opening up possibilities of interpretation that might otherwise not have been so evident. If the "reading" of an exegete is a "great" reading, if it plumbs depths unsuspected by the reader, it becomes a guide to the reconstruction of reality—much, say, as Albert Guerard's "reading" of Conrad changed the "reality" of *The Secret Sharer* from an adventure to a psychological story. Should we object then that the thoughtful man of letters is set wondering about the limits of or the boundlessness of interpretation?

Grant that it is utter deconstructionist vanity, say, to elevate Barthes's *S/Z* to the same artistic status as Balzac's *Sarrasine,* which it is intended to explicate. Yet, Barthes (like Odo of Cluny or any other famous or obscure medieval exegete) does explicate the codes by which our "effort after meaning" is guided in the process of reading *Sar-*

rasine. He is not trying to undermine our faith in meaning-fulness (any more than medieval scholars by proposing multiple interpretations of Scripture were trying to undermine faith in Scripture). After all, Angelom of Luxeuil had eight levels of interpretation, Odo of Cluny seven, and Barthes has only five. My diagnosis—given in the spirit of a student of human cognition—is that there is no end to belief in meaning and reality. We thirst after them. We are natural ontologists but reluctant epistemologists. The intellectual news in any generation is not that there *are* meaning and reality, but that it is extraordinarily difficult to figure out how they are achieved. The ontology, I would want to argue, looks after itself. It is epistemology that needs cultivating.

It requires the most expensive education to shake a reader's faith in the incarnateness of meaning in a novel or poem. And one would need postgraduate folly to believe that a commentary on Milton's *Paradise Lost* is the same stuff as the poem itself. We do not "suspend disbelief" in Coleridge's sense when reading, say, Christopher Ricks's splendid annotations. Ricks gets no license from us. He must go the rough route of epistemology. Even his most reasonable proposals run a logical gamut to which I, for one, would never subject Satan in reading the poem. Yes, Satan *is;* Ricks's notes *signify*.

I think it is the literary politics to which deconstruction is put that is quite properly bothering George Steiner, not the rather philosophically harebrained perspectivalism that is now living out its sunset in Paris and New Haven and in the intellectual suburbs. Tzvetan Todorov's interesting and amusing essay-review of Robert Scholes's book helps make that clearer.

Todorov sets out to explore (with demurrers for his innocence on the subject) the American critical scene. "Up until—roughly speaking—1968, the majority of American critics seemed preoccupied by one crucial question: 'What does this text mean?' Confronted with a text upon which they were to comment, they held at least one conviction in common, namely that the most important thing to do was to determine as accurately as possible what the text was trying to say." There was disagreement about the best way to accomplish this end: whether by study of the author, through stylistics, through genre analysis, whatever. Structuralism changed the program little: its tools were new means to answering the old question, whether the tools of Propp's *Morphology,* of Russian Formalism, of Lévi-Strauss's contrastive analyses, or out of Northrop Frye's or Eliade's toolkits.

The arrival of post-structuralism on the American scene made the old question irrelevant. In one of its forms, deconstruction, the answer to the question of what a text meant was "nothing." In the other of its forms, pragmaticism, the answer was "anything." The nihilist response of deconstruction was, of course, based on the primitive axiom that since it is impossible to know the world directly, only discourse exists, and discourse can only refer to other discourse—a denial of perception, and of any other form of outside-the-text reference. In this dispensation, as Todorov notes, we are "liberated" from the empirical object. As if this were not enough, there is a second claim: discourse is itself riven with contradictions and, in any case, its meanings are underdetermined. No comfort there in the search for univocal meanings. Thirdly (and obviously, given the first two assertions), since no discourse is free of contradiction, "there is no reason to favour one kind above another, or to choose one value in preference to another." Faith and reason, then, are equally baseless, both stem from a common root—a religious root at that. As Todorov says, "they [the deconstructionists] speak of reason itself as a reincarnation of God, no less, sweeping away in a single penstroke several centuries of struggle." Or bunch all of them together under the rubric of "power," which puts logic, God, and the police force on an equal footing.

"The other main variant of 'post-structuralism,' pragmaticism (whose most prominent representative is Stanley Fish), obtains results which are considerably less monotonous. Its central hypotheses are as follows: A text means nothing in and of itself; it is the reader who gives it meaning." And since the text has no stable meaning of its own, it is the reader and the critic and, finally, an "interpretive community" that make stable meanings. Todorov (who comes equipped with the training of a linguist, whatever else he may have turned his hand to) indignantly rejects both the idea that language itself is little better than a Rorschach into which the reader projects meanings *ad libitum,* and the claim that readers can read in any which way given the constraints imposed upon them as language users. And his indignation extends as well to the pragmaticist notion that critical and interpretive writing should be interesting rather than accurate—a corollary to the view that readers rather than texts provide stability of meaning, meaning thus being the prize gained (at least *pro tem*) by that reader offering the most "interesting" interpretation in the ever-renewed auction constituted by the interpretative community. Obviously, nobody ever retires the prize. To Todorov (as to Scholes) this is an Orwellian universe out of *Nineteen Eighty-Four,* with the Party as the interpretative community.

Given such a Nietzschean perspectivalism, the only interesting question to ask about an utterance or poem or text is *why* it was said or written. Questions like "What does it mean?" or "Is it true?" become transmuted into "Why did (s)he say that?" The psychoanalytic approach to such a question was too private, too rooted in individual idiosyncrasy, too lacking in a sense of human history and the broader social condition to provide a program for literary criticism and interpretation. On Todorov's reckoning, then, the ground was ready and vacant for the Marxist critic.

"What interests Marxist criticism is neither the book as a representation of the world nor the book as a statement about the world; instead, it is the world (or rather a fraction of it) as the origin of the book." Since the class struggle is at the center of its value system, any notion of universal or "inter-class" values or meanings is anathema. Any quest for values or for meanings is reduced to the defense of a particular group's interest, and since only the "socialist transformation of society" is accepted as a universal, what is good is what contributes to that transformation, no matter what people might feel about it. History, particularly the history of conflict, was to take the place of reason as a means of establishing meaning, and meaning is not "what" but "what for." On any abstract reckoning, of course, the two schools—deconstruction and Marxism—should be at daggers drawn. What brings them together, Todorov concludes, is that "both are fighting a common enemy, and that enemy's name is humanism—that is, . . . the attempt to ground science and ethics in reason, and to practise them in a universal way." He ends with a spoof. "Who said that 'the idea of justice in itself is an idea which in effect has been invented and put to work in different societies as an instrument of a certain political and economic power or as a weapon against that power'? No, not Terry Eagleton, but Michel Foucault."

So let us pick up again the thread of the earlier discussion, and see whether Todorov and Steiner can be encompassed in a common frame. Both reject the view that there is no reality, no meaning that is extratextual. Todorov, like Steiner, expresses faith in reason. Todorov offers a "critical humanism" as an equivalent to Steiner's act of transcendence or moral commitment to "meaning-fulness": as Todorov puts it, "a relationship between literature and the world must be recognized." Both believe that some interpretations are more right than others, some evaluative criticisms more appropriate. Todorov cites with approval Scholes's conclusion: "the whole point of my argument is that we must open the way between the literary or verbal text and the social text in which we live." Each of them in his own way asserts that the reader creates a world out of meanings he finds *in* a text and that there are universal modes of reason and valuation that the reader brings to bear in doing so, just as there are meanings "incarnate" in the text. For both Todorov and Steiner, language and its products—poetry, fiction, history, and the sciences—function to open the world for the reader rather than, as in Marxist dogma, to close it down as a means to further the interest of one group against another.

I have argued in earlier chapters for a constructivist view of reality: that we cannot know an aboriginal reality; that there is none; that any reality we create is based on a transmutation of some prior "reality" that we have taken as given. We construct many realities, and do so from differing intentions. But we do not construct them out of Rorschach blots, but out of the myriad forms in which we structure experience—whether the experience of the senses (and again, it would take an extraordinarily refined education to persuade one that one's perceptions do not "exist"), the deeply symbolically encoded experience we gain through interacting with our social world, or the vicarious experience we achieve in the act of reading. As I tried to demonstrate in Chapter 7, it is *not* the case that a constructivist philosophy of mind (or of literary meaning) disarms one either ontologically or ethically. Interpretations, whether of text or of world experience, can be judged for their rightness. Their rightness, however, is not to be reckoned by correspondence to an aboriginal "real" world "out there." For such a "real world" is not only indeterminate epistemologically, but even empty as an act of faith. Rather, meaning (or "reality," for in the end the two are indistinguishable) is an enterprise that reflects human intentionality and cannot be judged for its rightness independently of it. But "world making," in Nelson Goodman's sense (see Chapter 7), starting as it does from a prior world that we take as given, is constrained by the nature of the world version with which we begin the remaking. It is not a relativistic picnic. If there are meanings "incarnate" in the world (or in the text with which we start) we transform them in the act of accepting them into our transformed world, and that transformed world then becomes the world with which others start, or that we then offer. In the end, it is the transaction of meaning by human beings, human beings armed with reason and buttressed by the faith that sense can be made and remade, that makes human culture—and by culture, I do not mean surface consensus.

I have tried to make the case that the function of literature as art is to open us to dilemmas, to the hypothetical, to the range of possible worlds that a text can refer to. I have used the term "to subjunctivize," to render the world less fixed, less banal, more susceptible to recreation. Literature subjunctivizes, makes strange, renders the obvious less so, the unknowable less so as well, matters of value more open to reason and intuition. Literature, in this spirit, is an instrument of freedom, lightness, imagination, and yes, reason. It is our only hope against the long gray night.

Unlike Steiner and Todorov, I am *not* alarmed by deconstruction and pragmaticism. I see both these schools as excesses of a virtue, excesses distorted by both fear and vanity, yet reflecting the revolution of our times—in science, philosophy, and politics—the revolution that has led us from concern with *what* we know to a preoccupation with *how* we know. Their excesses have already assured their corruption, and they exist now in faddish enclaves with a dwindling clientele, addicted more to slogans than to substance.

I deeply respect George Steiner's desire to save us from our epistemic excesses, but I do not think that a moral act of transcendence (or any other form of wearing the white ribbon) will suffice. What will see us through is the writing of poems and novels that help perpetually to recreate the world, and the writing of criticism and interpretation that celebrate the varied ways in which human beings search for meaning and for its incarnation in reality—or better, in such rich realities as we can create.

I also respect Tzvetan Todorov's concern about the politically motivated antihumanism that is "pop deconstruction." But Marxist rhetoric that uses empty relativism as a base for "critical theory" risks its own destruction by breeding a boredom that only the devout can bear. The danger to critical humanism comes, I think, not from this hybrid (for it has no intellectual firepower and little emotional appeal in its own right), but from the kind of alienation that is comforted by the doctrine that everything is equally unknowable, equally meaningless, equally absurd. Whenever the weather comes in that form, it leads to local squalls. And if there are enough of them, they can be dangerous. It is only in that kind of atmosphere that deconstructionist know-nothingness joined with Marxist dogmatism can be a force. Again, all that one can hope for is an open market. Boredom has always played more of a role in human history than we are prepared to admit. And we should never underrate the boredom induced by empty ideas pretentiously paraded.

Appendix: A Reader's Retelling of "Clay" by James Joyce

Joyce's Actual Text

1. The matron had given her leave to go out as soon as the women's tea was over and Maria looked forward to her evening out.
2. The kitchen was spick and span: the cook said you could see yourself in the big copper boilers.
3. The fire was nice and bright and on one of the side-tables were four very big barmbracks.
4. These barmbracks seemed uncut; but if you went closer you would see that they had been cut into long thick even slices and were ready to be handed round at tea.
5. Maria had cut them herself.

6. Maria was a very, very small person indeed but she had a very long nose and a very long chin.
7. She talked a little through her nose, always soothingly: *Yes, my dear,* and *No, my dear.*
8. She was always sent for when the women quarrelled over their tubs and always succeeded in making peace.
9. One day the matron had said to

The Reader's Virtual Text

The story goes like this: Uh, he starts out by, uh, telling us that, um, the lady named Maria will be um waiting for, is waiting for the women to come for a tea party type of thing and she also knows that after the tea party, about a little before seven she'll be able to go out um, into town, for, like, a night of shopping. And, um, he says that there's a nice fire burning in the room

Actual Text	*Virtual Text*

her: —Maria, you are a veritable peace-maker!

10. And the sub-matron and two of the Board ladies had heard the compliment.
11. And Ginger Mooney was always saying what she wouldn't do to the dummy who had charge of the irons if it wasn't for Maria.
12. Everyone was so fond of Maria.

13. The women would have their tea at six o'clock and she would be able to get away before seven.
14. From Ballsbridge to the Pillar, twenty minutes; from the Pillar to Drumcondra, twenty minutes; and twenty minutes to buy the things.
15. She would be there before eight.
16. She took out her purse with the silver clasps and read again the words *A Present from Belfast*.
17. She was very fond of that purse because Joe had brought it to her five years before when he and Alphy had gone to Belfast on a Whit-Monday trip.
18. In the purse were two half-crowns and some coppers.
19. She would have five shillings clear after paying tram fare.
20. What a nice evening they would have, all the children singing!
21. Only she hoped that Joe wouldn't come in drunk.
22. He was so different when he took any drink.

23. Often he had wanted her to go and live with them; but she would have felt herself in the way (though Joe's wife was ever so nice with her) and she had become accustomed to the life of the laundry.

Actual Text

24. Joe was a good fellow.
25. She had nursed him and Alphy too; and Joe used often say: —Mamma is mamma but Maria is my proper mother.

26. After the break-up at home the boys had got her that position in the *Dublin by Lamplight* laundry, and she liked it.
27. She used to have such a bad opinion of Protestants but now she thought they were very nice people, a little quiet and serious, but still very nice people to live with.
28. Then she had her plants in the conservatory and she liked looking after them.
29. She had lovely ferns and wax-plants and, whenever anyone came to visit her, she always gave the visitor one or two slips from her conservatory.
30. There was one thing she didn't like and that was the tracts on the walls; but the matron was such a nice person to deal with, so genteel.

31. When the cook told her everything was ready she went into the women's room and began to pull the big bell.
32. In a few minutes the women began to come in by twos and threes, wiping their steaming hands in their petticoats and pulling down the sleeves of their blouses over their red steaming arms.
33. They settled down before their huge mugs which the cook and the dummy filled up with hot tea, already mixed with milk and sugar in huge tin cans.
34. Maria superintended the distribu-

Virtual Text

and she's waiting there and the ladies are in the other room, and when the cook is ready, he tells her to go on into the other room and she rings this big bell and everybody starts coming in. And, he said earlier that there were four barmbracks on the corner table and it didn't look like they were sliced but if you went closer, he said you could see that they were sliced into evenly cut long pieces and it was her job to, ah, make sure that everybody got their share of their barmbracks, prob'ly around four slices each. And, she did that and um everybody liked Maria 'cause she was always the one

Actual Text	*Virtual Text*
tion of the barmbrack and saw that every woman got her four slices. 35. There was a great deal of laughing and joking during the meal. 36. Lizzie Fleming said Maria was sure to get the ring and, though Fleming had said that for so many Hallow Eves, Maria had to laugh and say she didn't want any ring or man either; and when she laughed her grey-green eyes sparkled with disappointed shyness and the tip of her nose nearly met the tip of her chin. 37. Then Ginger Mooney lifted up her mug of tea and proposed Maria's health while all the other women clattered with their mugs on the table, and said she was sorry she hadn't a sup of porter to drink it in. 38. And Maria laughed again till the tip of her nose nearly met the tip of her chin and till her minute body nearly shook itself asunder because she knew that Mooney meant well though, of course, she had the notions of a common woman.	who um, she was like the judge between disputes, she always settled arguments and stuff and everybody really liked her. And, um, after tea, um after tea they all sat around still talking and joking and, and, she sat around for a little while and when, he said that when she laughed, that the tip of her nose almost touched the tip of her chin because she had a very long pointy nose and a very long chin. And, then, um, she decides that she has stayed long enough and goes and changes into her nice clothes, 'cause right now she's in her working clothes.
39. But wasn't Maria glad when the women had finished their tea and the cook and the dummy had begun to clear away the tea-things! 40. She went into her little bedroom and, remembering that the next morning was a mass morning, changed the hand of the alarm from seven to six. 41. Then she took off her working skirt and her house-boots and laid her best skirt out on the bed and her tiny dress-boots beside the foot of the bed. 42. She changed her blouse too and, as she stood before the mirror, she thought of how she used to dress for mass on Sunday morning when she was a young girl; and she looked with	So, she takes off her big boots, and she takes off her apron, and she goes and she um she's standing in front of the mirror and he tells you that she's a very small person, well, he told you that earlier, but he, you know, he emphasizes how small she is, but he says that she has a very nice dainty body, it's very neat and it's not, it's not fat or anything, and, and that, even though she's kind of old, still, she still likes her body. And, she changes, and then she remembers how she used to dress um when she was little how she used to dress for Sunday mass, and she dresses, and then she dresses, puts on her nice dress, she puts on her nice

Actual Text	*Virtual Text*
quaint affection at the diminutive body which she had so often adorned. 43. In spite of its years she found it a nice tidy little body.	little boots, and she goes on the tram. She figures out how long it'll take to get to where she wants to go, and she takes the tram and she says that um, there's only one seat left in the corner, so she goes and sits in the corner, and her feet since she's so small, her feet barely even touch the floor, and she rides the tram to one place, and then she has to take another tram, to another place, and finally she gets out and by this time you've learned that it's . . . it's Halloween night, or it will be soon; it's only about, about seven . . . thirty, now.
44. When she got outside the streets were shining with rain and she was glad of her old brown raincloak. 45. The tram was full and she had to sit on the little stool at the end of the car, facing all the people, with her toes barely touching the floor. 46. She arranged in her mind all she was going to do and thought how much better it was to be independent and to have your own money in your pocket. 47. She hoped they would have a nice evening. 48. She was sure they would but she could not help thinking what a pity it was Alphy and Joe were not speaking. 49. They were always falling out now but when they were boys together they used to be the best of friends: but such was life.	
50. She got out of her tram at the Pillar and ferreted her way quickly among the crowds. 51. She went into Downes's cakeshop but the shop was so full of people that it was a long time before she could get herself attended to. 52. She bought a dozen of mixed penny cakes, and at last came out of the shop laden with a big bag. 53. Then she thought what else would she buy: she wanted to buy something really nice. 54. They would be sure to have plenty of apples and nuts. 55. It was hard to know what to buy and all she could think of was cake.	And it's Halloween, so she's going to, um, a pastry to buy little cookies and stuff for, ah, for a friend of hers whose name is Joe . . . and, when she gets to the store where they're selling the cookies, she pulls out her purse, and it says: *A Present from Belfast,* inside, 'cause it was a present from Joe . . . a long time ago. And she remembers when, when he gave it to her and so, then she pays the lady for the ah, some penny cakes and she buys a dozen penny cakes, and then she thinks what else she wants to buy. So, then she goes to a, um, she wants to buy a piece of plumcake . . . for, yeah, a piece of plumcake for, for the, um,

Actual Text	*Virtual Text*
56. She decided to buy some plumcake but Downes's plumcake had not enough almond icing on top of it so she went over to a shop in Henry Street.	for Joe and for Joe's wife, (two words indistinct due to fire sirens outside window) . . . um, she's, she's gonna buy it at this store, and then she remembers that the, this store doesn't put enough almond icing on the plumcake, . . . it's either not enough or too much, I don't remember which.
57. Here she was a long time in suiting herself and the stylish young lady behind the counter, who was evidently a little annoyed by her, asked her was it wedding-cake she wanted to buy. 58. That made Maria blush and smile at the young lady; but the young lady took it all very seriously and finally cut a thick slice of plumcake, parcelled it up and said: —Two-and-four, please.	So, then she goes to this other store where she knows and she buys a piece of plumcake and she's, um, then she takes the tram again, to . . . Joe's house, and on the tram she meets a guy, an old man, who, um, who's the only one—well, when she goes on the tram, there's no seats at all, she's forced to stand, and she's kind of appalled that none of the young men will give up their seats to a lady, but there's an old man, sitting, who relinquishes his seat, and she sits down
59. She thought she would have to stand in the Drumcondra tram because none of the young men seemed to notice her but an elderly gentleman made room for her. 60. He was a stout gentleman and he wore a brown hard hat; he had a square red face and a greyish moustache.	and they talk,
61. Maria thought he was a colonel-looking gentleman and she reflected how much more polite he was than the young men who simply stared straight before them. 62. The gentleman began to chat with her about Hallow Eve and the rainy weather. 63. He supposed the bag was full of good things for the little ones and said it was only right that the youngsters should enjoy themselves while they were young.	and um, he sees that she's bought some cakes and some pie and stuff and he says, since it's Halloween, he says, you know, it's good that the children should enjoy themselves on Halloween while they're still young, and they then they talk, they talk for a while while she's on, on the tram.

Actual Text	*Virtual Text*
64. Maria agreed with him and favoured him with demure nods and hems. 65. He was very nice with her, and when she was getting out at the Canal Bridge she thanked him and bowed, and he bowed to her and raised his hat and smiled agreeably; and while she was going up along the terrace, bending her tiny head under the rain, she thought how easy it was to know a gentleman even when he has a drop taken.	And he's very nice, and when she has to get off, he lifts his hat and says Goodbye, and, and, you know, she's very happy that he's such a nice man.
66. Everybody said: *O, here's Maria!* when she came to Joe's house. 67. Joe was there, having come home from business, and all the children had their Sunday dresses on. 68. There were two big girls in from next door and games were going on. 69. Maria gave the bag of cakes to the eldest boy, Alphy, to divide and Mrs Donnelly said it was too good of her to bring such a big bag of cakes and made all the children say: —Thanks, Maria. 70. But Maria said she had brought something special for papa and mamma, something they would be sure to like, and she began to look for her plumcake.	And she goes to Joe's house, and everybody loves Maria, 'cause she's such a nice lady, and, um, the kids like her, and Joe likes her and Joe's wife really likes her, and she remembers that Joe's wife had asked her once to, um, I mean Joe had asked her once to live there, and she had become very used to to living there, I mean she had become very accustomed to . . . well, she had thought about it because she . . . the position that she had with the matron was like, um, doing the laundry and chores and stuff I guess, so she had thought about it and since Joe's wife liked her so much she had seriously considered it, but she thought she'd be pretty much in the way, so she goes there and she gives the kids their little penny cakes and they're very happy, and she gives . . . and then she's gonna give Joe and his wife the piece of plumcake
71. She tried in Downes's bag and then in the pockets of her raincloak and then on the hall-stand but nowhere could she find it. 72. Then she asked all the children had any of them eaten it—by mistake,	but she realizes that she can't find it anywhere,

Actual Text

of course—but the children all said no and looked as if they did not like to eat cakes if they were to be accused of stealing.

73. Everybody had a solution for the mystery and Mrs Donnelly said it was plain that Maria had left it behind her in the tram.

74. Maria, remembering how confused the gentleman with the greyish moustache had made her, coloured with shame and vexation and disappointment.

75. At the thought of the failure of her little surprise and of the two and fourpence she had thrown away for nothing she nearly cried outright.

76. But Joe said it didn't matter and made her sit down by the fire.

77. He was very nice with her.

78. He told her all that went on in his office, repeating for her a smart answer which he had made to the manager.

79. Maria did not understand why Joe laughed so much over the answer he had made but she said that the manager must have been a very overbearing person to deal with.

80. Joe said he wasn't so bad when you know how to take him, that he was a decent sort so long as you didn't rub him the wrong way.

81. Mrs Donnelly played the piano for the children and they danced and sang.

82. Then the two next-door girls handed round the nuts.

83. Nobody could find the nutcrackers and Joe was nearly getting cross over it and asked how did they expect Maria to crack nuts without a nutcracker.

Virtual Text

and she's so sad that she almost starts crying, and she realizes that the man who had been so nice to her probably stole the piece of plumcake from her. She gets very sad.

Actual Text	*Virtual Text*
84. But Maria said she didn't like nuts and that they weren't to bother about her. 85. Then Joe asked would she take a bottle of stout and Mrs Donnelly said there was port wine too in the house if she would prefer that. 86. Maria said she would rather they didn't ask her to take anything: but Joe insisted.	
87. So Maria let him have his way and they sat by the fire talking over old times and Maria thought she would put in a good word for Alphy. 88. But Joe cried that God might strike him stone dead if ever he spoke a word to his brother again and Maria said she was sorry she had mentioned the matter. 89. Mrs Donnelly told her husband it was a great shame for him to speak that way of his own flesh and blood but Joe said that Alphy was no brother of his and there was nearly being a row on the head of it. 90. But Joe said he would not lose his temper on account of the night it was and asked his wife to open some more stout. 91. The two next-door girls had arranged some Hallow Eve games and soon everything was merry again. 92. Maria was delighted to see the children so merry and Joe and his wife in such good spirits.	But then, Joe breaks out with the wine and the beer and stuff and they start being merry, and they start, the kids start playing games and, before they play games, Maria said to Joe that, he should really make up with his brother Alphy, but Joe gets very angry and he says that if he should speak to his brother again, that God might strike him down but with, a bolt of lightning. And, um, Maria says that she's sorry she brought up the subject and Joe says, you know, since it's such a nice night, I won't get angry about it, but, you know, he doesn't, he's not really happy that she brought it up.
93. The next-door girls put some saucers on the table and then led the children up to the table, blindfold. 94. One got the prayer-book and the other three got the water; and when one of the next-door girls got the ring Mrs Donnelly shook her finger at the blushing girl as much as to say: *O, I know all about it!*	And, then they play a game where they blindfold Maria and um the two girls from next door . . . put out little saucers and little things on the saucers

Actual Text	*Virtual Text*
95. They insisted then on blindfolding Maria and leading her up to the table to see what she would get; and, while they were putting on the bandage, Maria laughed and laughed again till the tip of her nose nearly met the tip of her chin.	and they blindfold Maria
96. They led her up to the table amid laughing and joking and she put her hand out in the air as she was told to do.	
97. She moved her hand about here and there in the air and descended on one of the saucers. 98. She felt a soft wet substance with her finger and was surprised that nobody spoke or took off her bandage. 99. There was a pause for a few seconds; and then a great deal of scuffling and whispering. 100. Somebody said something about the garden, and at last Mrs Donnelly said something very cross to one of the next-door girls and told her to throw it out at once: that was no play. 101. Maria understood that it was wrong that time and so she had to do it over again: and this time she got the prayer-book.	and she has to put her hand on one of the saucers and whatever's there um means something, supposedly. And she does it the first time, and she feels something wet, and mushy, kind of I guess, and everybody's whispering and making, you know, strange sounds, then someone says something about the garden, and then Joe's wife says, you know, that . . . tells the girls that that's not very funny, and some . . . you know, and Maria has to do it again, and the next time she gets um the Bible . . . I think, yeah, the Bible, and they tell her that by the end of the year, uh, she will enter a convent cause she got the Bible, then, ah, then, the, since they've had enough of that game, they start talking again, and Joe's so happy that, that Maria came and Maria says that this is the nicest Joe's ever been to us, to her . . . She doesn't say it, but she thinks it.
102. After that Mrs Donnelly played Miss McCloud's Reel for the children and Joe made Maria take a glass of wine. 103. Soon they were all quite merry again and Mrs Donnelly said Maria would enter a convent before the year was out because she had got the prayer-book. 104. Maria had never seen Joe so nice to her as he was that night, so full of pleasant talk and reminiscences.	

Actual Text	*Virtual Text*
105. She said they were all very good to her.	
106. At last the children grew tired and sleepy and Joe asked Maria would she not sing some little song before she went, one of the old songs.	And, um, Joe, asks Joe and his wife, ask Maria to sing a song,
107. Mrs Donnelly said *Do, please, Maria!* and so Maria had to get up and stand beside the piano.	
108. Mrs Donnelly bade the children be quiet and listen to Maria's song.	
109. Then she played the prelude and said *Now, Maria!* and Maria, blushing very much, began to sing in a tiny quavering voice.	
110. She sang *I Dreamt that I Dwelt,* and when she came to the second verse she sang again: *I dreamt that I dwelt in marble halls / With vassals and serfs at my side / And of all who assembled within those walls / That I was the hope and the pride.*	so Maria sings this song called, um, *I Dreamt that I Dwelt,* and it's a song about her being ahm, a knight in a marble hall and having vassals and, um, having a lot of money and that, being glad that um the person who loves her loves her (cough) anyway, in spite of all her money and stuff, I mean, even though she has a lot of money, but that she loves her anyway,
111. *I had riches too great to count, could boast / Of a high ancestral name, / But I also dreamt, which pleased me most, / That you loved me still the same.*	
112. But no one tried to show her her mistake; and when she had ended her song Joe was very much moved.	
113. He said that there was no time like the long ago and no music for him like poor old Balfe, whatever other people might say; and his eyes filled up so much with tears that he could not find what he was looking for and in the end he had to ask his wife to tell him where the corkscrew was.	and Joe starts crying, and he's crying so hard he can't find what he's looking for, so he has to ask someone else to find him the corkscrew. And that's the end of the story.

Notes

1. Approaching the Literary

p. 3 Czeslaw Milosz, *The Witness of Poetry,* The Charles Eliot Norton Lectures 1981–82 (Cambridge, Mass.: Harvard University Press, 1983). Quotations from p. 3.

Sigmund Freud, "The Poet and the Daydream," in *The Collected Papers* (New York: Collier Books, 1963).

p. 4 Roman Jakobson, "Linguistics and Poetics," in *Style in Language,* ed. T. Sebeok (Cambridge, Mass.: M.I.T. Press, 1960).

Vladimir Propp, *The Morphology of the Folktale* (Austin: University of Texas Press, 1968).

Kenneth Burke, *The Grammar of Motives* (New York: Prentice-Hall, 1945); see also Dennis Donoghue's evaluation of Burke's work in the *New York Review of Books,* Sept. 21, 1985.

Roland Barthes, *S/Z: An Essay* (New York: Hill and Wang, 1974).

I. A. Richards, *Practical Criticism: A Study of Literary Judgment,* rpt. ed. (New York: Harcourt, Brace, 1935).

p. 5 Nicholas of Lyra (c.1265–1349) was a Franciscan whose works were widely known in the fourteenth and fifteenth centuries. His most famous works were two commentaries on the Bible, *Postilla litteralis* (1322–31) and *Postilla mystica sen moralis* (1339). Born in Lire in Normandy, he was the subject of a pun, "lire et délire," that caught nicely the distinction between his literal readings and his mystical ones. He is characterized in the eleventh edition of the *Encyclopedia Britannica* as having had "a very independent attitude toward traditional interpretation, and a remarkable historical and critical sense."

p. 6 A. Warren and R. Wellek, *Theory of Literature* (New York: Harcourt, Brace, 1949).

Wolfgang Iser, *The Act of Reading* (Baltimore: Johns Hopkins University Press, 1978); see also his *The Implied Reader* (Johns Hopkins, 1974).

p. 7 Anthony Burgess, *ReJoyce* (New York: Norton, 1965).

Paul Ricoeur, *Time and Narrative* (Chicago: University of Chicago Press, 1983).

Frank Kermode, "Secrets and Narrative Sequence," in W. J. T. Mitchell, ed., *On Narrative* (Chicago: University of Chicago Press, 1981).

p. 8 G. T. Fechner, *Buechlein von Leben nach dem Tode* (1836); for further discussion see E. G. Boring, *History of Experimental Psychology* (New York: Appleton Century Crofts, 1950).

Jerome Bruner, *On Knowing: Essays for the Left Hand* (Cambridge, Mass.: Harvard University Press, 1962).

p. 9 For a general account of work on story grammars, see Jean Mandler, *Stories, Scripts, and Scenes: Aspects of Schema Theory* (Hillsdale, N.J.: L. Erlbaum Associates, 1984). See also Roger Shank and Robert Abelson on the theory of scripts and scenarios in *Scripts, Plans, Goals and Understanding* (Erlbaum, 1977). A particularly seminal article in the literature in story grammars is D. E. Rumelhart, "Notes on a Schema for Stories," in D. G. Bobrow and A. Collins, eds., *Representation and Understanding* (New York: Academic Press, 1975).

2. Two Modes of Thought

p. 11 Parts of this chapter appeared as "Narrative and Paradigmatic Modes of Thought," in the 1985 Yearbook of the National Society for the Study of Education, *Learning and Teaching: The Ways of Knowing.*

p. 12 Karl Popper, *Objective Knowledge: An Evolutionary Approach* (Oxford: Clarendon Press, 1972).

Richard Rorty, *Philosophy and the Mirror of Nature* (Princeton: Princeton University Press, 1979).

p. 14 Paul Ricoeur, *Time and Narrative* (Chicago: University of Chicago Press, 1983).

W. V. O. Quine, "Review of Nelson Goodman's *Ways of Worldmaking*," *New York Review of Books* 25 (Nov. 23, 1978).

p. 15 William James, *The Varieties of Religious Experience: A Study in Human Nature; being the Gifford Lectures on natural religion delivered at Edinburgh in 1901–2* (New York: Longmans, Green, 1902).

S. L. Washburn, "One Hundred Years of Biological Anthropology," in J. O. Brew, ed., *One Hundred Years of Anthropology* (Cambridge, Mass.: Harvard University Press, 1968).

G. Polya, *How to Solve It: A New Aspect of Mathematical Method,* 2nd ed. (Princeton: Princeton University Press, 1971).

The reader may well ask how I would characterize the difference between narrative "at its far reach" as an art form, and the ordinary narratives that people offer in answer to such questions as "What have you been up to?" I think the question is better postponed until later in the chapter when I consider the "subjunctivation" process of great narrative—the means whereby it creates not only a story but also a sense of its contingent and uncertain variants.

p. 16 Victor Turner, *From Ritual to Theater* (New York: New York Performing Arts Journal Publications, 1982).

Tzvetan Todorov, *The Poetics of Prose* (Ithaca: Cornell University Press, 1977).

Hayden White, "The Value of Narrativity in the Representation of Reality," in W. J. T. Mitchell, ed., *On Narrative* (Chicago: University of Chicago Press, 1981).

Vladimir Propp, *The Morphology of the Folktale* (Austin: University of Texas Press, 1968).

Barbara Herrnstein-Smith, "Narrative Versions, Narrative Theories," in Mitchell, *On Narrative.*

p. 17 Julian Barnes, *Flaubert's Parrot* (New York: Knopf, 1985).

A. Michotte, *The Perception of Causality* (New York: Basic Books, 1963).

p. 18 Alan Leslie, "The Representation of Perceived Causal Connection" (D.Phil. Thesis, Department of Experimental Psychology, University of Oxford, 1979).

Fritz Heider and Marianne Simmel, "An Experimental Study of Apparent Behavior," *American Journal of Psychology* 57 (1944).

Judith Ann Stewart, "Perception of Animacy" (Ph.D. diss., University of Pennsylvania, 1982).

The test for an experiment on infant perception of animacy or apparent intention would parallel Leslie's procedure on infant perception of causality. He sums up his test as follows: "Following habituation, 27 week old infants recover interest more when the spatio-temporal direction of an apparently *causal* event is reversed than when the spatio-temporal direction of a highly similar but apparently *non-causal* event is reversed." The same test can be used for apparently animate and nonanimate displays. See Alan Leslie and Stephanie Keeble, "Six-month-old Infants Perceive Causality," Medical Research Council, Cognitive Development Unit, 17 Gordon Street, London, WC1H OAH.

p. 19 Roman Jakobson, "What Is Poetry?" in Jakobson, *Selected Writings,* ed. Stephen Rudy, vol. 3 (The Hague: Mouton, 1981).

Michel Leiris, *Manhood: A Journey from Childhood into the Fierce Order of Virility,* trans. Richard Howard (San Francisco: North Point Press, 1984).

p. 20 Kenneth Burke, *The Grammar of Motives* (New York: Prentice-Hall, 1945).

A. Greimas and J. Courtes, "The Cognitive Dimension of Narrative Discourse," *New Literary History* 7 (Spring 1976): 433–447.

p. 21 Frank Kermode, *The Sense of an Ending: Studies in the Theory of Fiction* (New York: Oxford University Press, 1967).

p. 22 Roman Jakobson, "Linguistics and Poetics," in *Style and Language,* ed. T. Sebeok (Cambridge, Mass.: M.I.T. Press, 1960).

For the Prague School see Peter Steiner, ed., *The Prague School: Selected Writings 1929–1946* (Austin: University of Texas Press, 1982); also see Jan Mukarovsky, *The Word and Verbal Art: Selected Essays,* trans. and ed. John Burbank and Peter Steiner (New Haven: Yale University Press, 1977).

The distinction is often made between "paradigmatic" and "syntagmatic" in studies of word association. The former refers to associations that are based on synonymy, hyponymy, or hyperonymy, such as *dog-canine, dog-dachshund,* and *dog-animal.* The latter refers to a coherence describable by permissible juxtaposition within a subject-predicate framework, such as *dog-runs,* or *dog-friendly.* It is a distinction that parallels Jakobson's vertical and horizontal axes in language, but Jakobson's intent went far beyond word association. Indeed, he went so far as to propose that the distinction could be used to distinguish between two forms of literary trope, the metaphoric (vertical) and the metonym (horizontal) and even between two types of aphasia, metaphoric (affecting word selection) and metonymic (affecting word combination).

p. 23 T. S. Eliot, "The Love Song of J. Alfred Prufrock," in *Collected Poems, 1909–1962* (New York: Harcourt, Brace and World, 1963), pp. 3–7.

Louis MacNeice, "The Sunlight on the Garden," in *Collected Poems, 1925–1948* (London: Faber and Faber, 1949).

p. 24 William Butler Yeats, "The Sorrow of Love," in *The Poems of W. B. Yeats,* ed. Richard J. Finneran (New York: Macmillan, 1983). See also R. Jakobson and S. Rudy, "Yeats' 'Sorrow of Love' Through the Years," in R. Jakobson, *Selected Writings,* III (The Hague: Mouton, 1981), p. 600.

Wolfgang Iser, *The Act of Reading* (Baltimore: Johns Hopkins University Press, 1978). Quotations from pp. 21, 61.

p. 26 W. H. Auden, "In Memory of W. B. Yeats (d. January 1939)."

H. P. Grice, "Logic and Conversation," in P. Cole and J. L. Morgan, eds., *Syntax and Semantics 3: Speech Acts* (New York: Academic Press, 1975); idem, "Presupposition and Conversational Implicature," in P. Cole, ed., *Radical Pragmatics* (New York: Academic Press, 1981).

p. 27 L. Karttunen and R. S. Peters, "Requiem for Presupposition," in *Proceedings of the Third Annual Meeting of the Berkeley Linguistics Society.* (Berkeley, 1977). For an excellent discussion of this work see Stephen Levinson, *Pragmatics* (Cambridge: Cambridge University Press: 1983), which also provides an excellent overview of the issues involved in the triggering of presuppositions.

Gerald Gazdar, *Pragmatics: Implicature, Presupposition, and Logical Form* (New York: Academic Press, 1979).

p. 28 Dan Sperber and Deirdre Wilson, "Mutual Knowledge and Relevance in Theories of Comprehension," in N. V. Smith, ed., *Mutual Knowledge* (London: Academic Press, 1982). Sperber and Wilson's account, of course, greatly refines the question of how much and what kind of mutual knowledge is needed to assure a mythologically instructed community.

Joseph Campbell, *The Hero with a Thousand Faces* (New York: Pantheon Books, 1949).

p. 29 Czeslaw Milosz, "Ars poetica?" in Milosz, *Bells in Winter* (New York: Ecco Press, 1978), p. 30.

Tzvetan Todorov, *The Poetics of Prose* (Ithaca: Cornell University Press, 1977).

p. 30 P. Ricoeur, *Time and Narrative* (Chicago: University of Chicago Press, 1983).

Todorov, *The Poetics of Prose,* p. 233.

p. 31 Martha Weigel, *Brothers of Light, Brothers of Blood: The Penitentes of the Southwest* (Albuquerque: University of New Mexico Press, 1976).

p. 33 Sir Frederick Bartlett, *Remembering: A Study in Experimental and Social Psychology* (Cambridge: Cambridge University Press, 1932).

p. 35 Clifford Geertz, *The Interpretation of Cultures* (New York: Basic Books, 1973).

Italo Calvino, *Invisible Cities,* trans. William Weaver (New York: Harcourt Brace Jovanovich, 1972). Quotations from pp. 86, 82.

p. 38 Aristotle, *Poetics.* An easily obtained complete edition is Richard McKeon, ed., *Introduction to Aristotle* (New York: Random House, Modern Library, 1947).

Seymour Chatman, *Story and Discourse: Narrative Structure in Fiction and Film* (Ithaca: Cornell University Press, 1978), p. 109.

Solomon Asch, "Forming Impressions of Personality," *Journal of Abnormal and Social Psychology* 41 (1946): 258–290.

Propp, *The Morphology of the Folktale.*

p. 39 Amélie Rorty, "A Literary Postscript: Characters, Persons, Selves, Individuals," in A. O. Rorty, ed., *The Identities of Persons* (Berkeley: University of California Press, 1976). Quotations from (in order) pp. 302, 303, 305, 306, 307, 308, 309, 313, 315.

p. 41 Lionel Trilling, review of David Riesman's *The Lonely Crowd,* rpt. in Trilling, *A Gathering of Fugitives* (Boston: Beacon Press, 1956).

p. 42 Dale Porter, *The Emergence of the Past: A Theory of Historical Explanation* (Chicago: University of Chicago Press, 1981).

W. Bryce Gallie, *Philosophy and the Historical Understanding* (New York: Schocken Books, 1968).

Isaiah Berlin, *Historical Inevitability* (London: Oxford University Press, 1955).

Arthur Danto, *Analytical Philosophy of History* (Cambridge: Cambridge University Press, 1965).

Louis Halphen, "The Coronation as the Expression of the Ideals of the Frankish Court," in Richard Sullivan, ed., *The Coronation of Charlemagne: What Did It Signify?* (Boston: D. C. Heath, 1959).

p. 43 White, "The Value of Narrativity."

For the reader not acquainted with contemporary work in literary theory, the following "K-ration" of books will provide an entry into the literature. W. J. T. Mitchell, ed., *On Narrative* (Chicago: University of Chicago Press, 1981); Seymour Chatman, *Story and Discourse: Narrative Structure in Fiction and Film* (Ithaca: Cornell University Press, 1978); Susan Suleiman and Inge Crosman, eds., *The Reader in the Text: Essays on Audience and Interpretation* (Princeton: Princeton University Press, 1980); Robert Scholes, *Semiotics and Interpretation* (New Haven: Yale University Press, 1982); Roland Barthes, *S/Z: An Essay* (New York: Hill and Wang, 1974); Jonathan Culler, *On Deconstruction: Theory and Criticism after Structuralism* (Ithaca: Cornell University Press, 1982); Iser, *The Act of Reading*; Jacques Derrida, *Writing and Difference* (Chicago: University of Chicago Press, 1978); Derrida, *Of Grammatology* (Baltimore: Johns Hopkins University Press, 1976). But any choice is arbitrary, and I cannot speak as a professional literary scholar or as an unbiased student. One could as well choose a completely different set of authors and find an interesting entry into this complex field—E. D. Hirsch, Frank Kermode, Bakhtin (particularly his *Dialogical Imagination*), Northrop Frye, or for that matter, Aristotle's *Poetics* or the essays of Harold Bloom, who finds his roots in quite a different tradition than most theorists and critics writing today.

3. Possible Castles

p. 45 Karl Popper, *Objective Knowledge: An Evolutionary Approach* (Oxford: Clarendon Press, 1972).

K. J. J. Hintikka, *Knowledge and Belief* (Ithaca: Cornell University Press, 1962).

Gordon Mills, *Hamlet's Castle: The Study of Literature as a Social Experience* (Austin: University of Texas Press, 1976).

p. 46 Two earlier papers of my own discuss the origins of these ideas about perception: "On Perceptual Readiness," *Psychological Review* 64 (1957): 123–152; and "Neural Mechanisms in Perception," *Psychological Review* 64 (1957): 340–358. A much more modern version of perceptual processing is to be found in David Marr, *Vision: A Computational Investigation in the Human Representation of Visual Information* (San Francisco: Freeman, 1982).

p. 47 George Miller, "The Magic Number Seven, Plus or Minus Two: Some Limits on Our Capacity for Processing Information," *Psychological Review* 63 (1956): 81–97.

Jerome Bruner and Leo Postman, "On the Perception of Incongruity: A Paradigm," *Journal of Personality* 18 (1949): 206–223.

Thomas Kuhn, *The Structure of Scientific Revolutions,* 2nd ed. (Chicago: University of Chicago Press, 1970).

p. 48 Ascher Shapiro, *Shape and Flow: The Fluid Dynamics of Drag* (Garden City, N.Y.: Anchor Books, 1961).

p. 49 Jerome Bruner, "Intention in the Structure of Action and Interaction," in L. Lipsitt, ed., *Advances in Infancy Research,* vol. 1 (Norwood, N.J.: Ablex, 1981).

Fritz Heider, *The Psychology of Interpersonal Relations* (New York: John Wiley, 1958).

p. 51 For a fuller account of this encounter with Niels Bohr, see my *In Search of Mind* (New York: Harper and Row, 1983).

p. 52 Manet's exclamation is often quoted and has become part of scholarly folklore. I must confess that I have not been able to find a source for it in spite of a vigorous search. My question is usually greeted with "Yes, of course, but where?"

4. The Transactional Self

p. 57 H. P. Grice, "Logic and Conversation," in P. Cole and J. L. Morgan, eds., *Syntax and Semantics 3: Speech Acts* (New York: Academic Press, 1975).

Dan Sperber and Deirdre Wilson, "Mutual Knowledge and Relevance in Theories of Comprehension," in N. V. Smith, ed., *Mutual Knowledge* (London: Academic Press, 1982).

Hilary Putnam, *Mind, Language and Reality,* vol. 2 (Cambridge: Cambridge University Press, 1975).

Colwyn Trevarthen, "Instincts for Human Understanding and for Cultural Cooperation: Their Development in Infancy," in M. von Cranach, K. Foppa, W. Lepenies, and D. Ploog, eds., *Human Ethology:*

Claims and Limits of a New Discipline (Cambridge: Cambridge University Press, 1979).

Max Scheler, *The Nature of Sympathy* (London: Routledge and Kegan Paul, 1954).

p. 58 For a fuller discussion of the impact of Fritz Heider's work, see E. E. Jones, "Major Developments in Social Psychology during the Last Five Decades," in G. Lindzey and E. Aronson, eds., *Handbook of Social Psychology,* 3rd ed. (New York: Random House, 1985), vol. 1.

Jerome Bruner and Renato Tagiuri, "The Perception of People," in Gardner Lindzey, ed., *Handbook of Social Psychology* (Reading, Mass.: Addison-Wesley, 1954).

p. 60 Jerome Bruner, "Learning How to Do Things with Words," in J. Bruner and A. Garton, eds., *Human Growth and Development,* Wolfson College Lectures (Oxford: Oxford University Press, 1976).

Michael Scaife and Jerome Bruner, "The Capacity for Joint Visual Attention in the Infant," *Nature* 253 (1975): 265–266.

The two classical discussions of "shifters" are John Lyons, *Semantics,* vols. 1 and 2 (Cambridge: Cambridge University Press, 1977); and Emile Benveniste, *Problems in General Linguistics* (Coral Gables, Fla.: University of Miami Press, 1971), chs. 18–23. For a more psychological discussion see Eve Clark, "From Gesture to Word: On the Natural History of Deixis in Language Acquisition," in Bruner and Garton, eds., *Human Growth and Development.*

For Mead's views see particularly George Herbert Mead, *Mind, Self, and Society* (Chicago: University of Chicago Press, 1934).

The "whipping boy" in this case is Jean Piaget's *The Child's Conception of Space* (London: Routledge and Kegan Paul, 1956).

p. 62 Joseph Greenberg, ed., *Universals of Language* (Cambridge, Mass.: M.I.T. Press, 1963); see also Greenberg, *Essays in Linguistics* (Chicago: University of Chicago Press, 1957).

Noam Chomsky, *Reflections on Language* (London: Temple Smith, 1976).

p. 63 Gareth Evans, *The Varieties of Reference,* ed. J. McDowell (Oxford: Oxford University Press, 1982); see also Charles Taylor's interesting review, "Dwellers in Egocentric Space," *Times Literary Supplement,* March 11, 1983.

p. 64 David Olson, "Language and Thought: Aspects of a Cognitive Theory of Semantics," *Psychological Review* 77 (1970): 257–273.

Ruth Weir, *Language in the Crib* (The Hague: Mouton, 1962).

The work of the New York Language Acquisition Group has not yet been published. It was presented in preliminary reports at the New York Child Language Group, November 1983, in papers delivered by Jerome Bruner, John Dore, Carol Feldman, Katherine Nelson, Daniel Stern, and Rita Watson.

For a discussion of constitutiveness as a "design feature" of language see Charles Hockett, *The View from Language: Selected Essays* (Athens, Ga.: University of Georgia Press, 1977). But of course the principal source for the idea of constitutiveness is John Austin's discussion of performatives in *How to Do Things with Words* (Oxford: Oxford University Press, 1962).

p. 65 Carol Feldman, "Epistemology and Ontology in Current Psychological Theory" (American Psychological Association Address, Sept. 1983); see also her "Thought from Language: The Linguistic Construction of Cognitive Representations," in Jerome Bruner and Helen Weinreich-Haste, eds., *Making Sense: The Child's Construction of the World* (London: Methuen, in press).

Clifford Geertz, *The Interpretation of Cultures* (New York: Basic Books, 1973).

Michelle Rosaldo, "Toward an Anthropology of Self and Feeling," in R. Schroeder and R. Le Vine, eds., *Culture Theory: Essays on Mind, Self, and Emotion* (Cambridge: Cambridge University Press, 1984), 137–158. Quotations from p. 140.

p. 66 Victor Turner, *From Ritual to Theatre* (New York: Performing Arts Journal Publications, 1982).

p. 67 For an account of the work of Ann Brown, J. R. Hayes, and David Perkins on metacognition, see S. F. Chipman, J. W. Segal, and R. Glaser, *Thinking and Learning Skills,* vol. 2 (Hillsdale, N.J.: Erlbaum, 1985), esp. chs. 14, 15, and 17.

For a review of studies on "repair" in child language, see Eve Clark, "Awareness of Language: Some Evidence from What Children Say and Do," in A. Sinclair, R. J. Jarvella, and W. J. M. Levelt, eds., *The Child's Conception of Language* (Berlin and New York: Springer-Verlag, 1978). For a particularly striking example of early repair, see chapter by Mary Louise Kasermann and Klaus Foppa, in Werner Deutsch, ed., *The Child's Construction of Language* (London: Academic Press, 1981).

p. 68 Katherine Nelson and J. Grundel, "At Morning It's Lunchtime: A Scriptal View of Children's Dialogue" (paper presented at the Conference on Dialogue, Language Development and Dialectical Research, University of Michigan, December 1977).

Margaret Donaldson, *Children's Minds* (New York: Norton, 1978).

Michelle Rosaldo, *Knowledge and Passion* (Stanford: Stanford University Press, 1980).

5. The Inspiration of Vygotsky

p. 70 An earlier version of this chapter was published under the title "Vygotsky: An Historical and Conceptual Perspective," in J. Wertsch, *Culture, Communication, and Cognition: Vygotskian Perspectives* (Cambridge: Cambridge University Press, 1985).

Edward Chace Tolman, "Cognitive Maps in Rats and Men," in Tolman, *Behavior and Psychological Man: Essays in Motivation and Learning* (Berkeley and Los Angeles: University of California Press, 1958).

There are available in English only two major works of Lev Vygotsky. One is *Thought and Language* (Cambridge, Mass.: M.I.T. Press, 1962); the other is *Mind in Society: The Development of Higher Psychological Processes,* ed. M. Cole, S. Scribner, V. John-Steiner, and E. Souderman (Cambridge, Mass.: Harvard University Press, 1978). A full translation of his papers is now in preparation under the editorship of Robert Rieber and a committee of Vygotsky scholars. Finally, a valuable source of material on Vygotsky's ideas is James Wertsch, ed., *Culture, Communication and Cognition* (Cambridge: Cambridge University Press, 1985).

p. 71 Raymond Bauer, *The New Man in Soviet Psychology* (Cambridge, Mass.: Harvard University Press, 1952).

A. N. Leontiev and A. R. Luria, "The Psychological Ideas of L. S. Vygotsky," in B. B. Wollman, ed., *Historical Roots of Contemporary Psychology* (New York: Harper and Row, 1968).

p. 74 Robert Hughes, *The Shock of the New* (New York: Knopf, 1981); see esp. pp. 81–97 for an account of Russian revolutionary avant-garde painters, designers, and "cultural politicians."

See particularly M. M. Bakhtin, *The Dialogic Imagination,* ed. Michael Holquist (Austin: University of Texas Press, 1981). An earlier book of Bakhtin's that provides an ideological background was published under his real name: V. N. Volosinov, *Marxism and the Philosophy of Lan-*

guage (New York and London: Seminar Press, 1973). See also Tzvetan Todorov, *Mikhail Bakhtin: The Dialogical Principle* (Minneapolis: University of Minnesota Press, 1984).

p. 75 David Wood, Jerome Bruner, and Gail Ross, "The Role of Tutoring in Problem-Solving." *Journal of Child Psychology and Psychiatry* 17 (1976): 89–100.

p. 76 For the inability or unwillingness of young "tutors" to give back the task to their younger charges, see Joan McLane, "Dyadic Problem Solving: A Comparison of Child-Child and Mother-Child Interaction" (Ph.D. diss., Northwestern University, 1981).

Barbara Tizard, M. Hughes, H. Carmichael, and G. Pinkerton, "Children's Questions and Adults' Answers" (paper presented to Section H, British Association for the Advancement of Science, Salford, England, 1981).

p. 77 Jerome Bruner, *Child's Talk* (New York: Norton, 1983).

Anat Ninio and Jerome Bruner, "The Achievement and Antecedents of Labeling," *Journal of Child Language* 5 (1978): 1–15.

Roger Brown, "Introduction," in Catherine Snow and Charles Ferguson, eds., *Talking to Children: Language Input and Acquisition* (Cambridge: Cambridge University Press, 1977).

6. Psychological Reality

p. 80 George Miller, "The Psycholinguists," *Encounter* 23, no. 1 (July 1964).

Carol Feldman and Stephen Toulmin, "Logic and the Theory of Mind," in *Nebraska Symposium on Motivation* (Lincoln: University of Nebraska Press, 1976).

p. 82 George Miller and Philip Johnson-Laird, *Language and Perception* (Cambridge, Mass.: Harvard University Press, 1976).

John Lyons, *Semantics,* vols. 1 and 2 (Cambridge: Cambridge University Press, 1977).

Charles Morris, *Signs, Language and Behavior* (New York: Prentice-Hall, 1946).

p. 83 Charles Fillmore, "The Case for Case," in E. Bach and R. T. Harms, eds., *Universals in Linguistic Theory* (New York: Holt, Rinehart and Winston, 1968).

Roger Brown, *A First Language: The Early Stages* (Cambridge, Mass.: Harvard University Press, 1973).

For the Prague School, see Peter Steiner, ed., *The Prague School: Selected Writings 1929–1946* (Austin: University of Texas Press, 1982).

Ulric Neisser, *Cognitive Psychology* (New York: Appleton Century Crofts, 1967).

p. 84 H. P. Grice, "Utterer's Meaning, Sentence Meaning, and Word Meaning," *Foundations of Language* 4 (1968): 1–18.

The decompositional view of meaning was most enthusiastically espoused by J. J. Katz and J. A. Fodor, "The Structure of a Semantic Theory," *Language* 39 (1963): 170–210; and by Manfred Bierwisch, "Semantics," in J. Lyons, ed., *New Horizons in Linguistics* (Baltimore: Penguin, 1970).

Oswald Ducrot, *Dire et ne pas dire: principes de semantique linguistique,* 2nd ed. (Paris: Hermann, 1980).

Peter Wason, "Response to Affirmative and Negative Binary Statements," *British Journal of Psychology* 52 (1961): 133–142; idem, "The Contexts of Plausible Denial," *Journal of Verbal Learning and Verbal Behavior* 4 (1965): 7–11.

p. 85 John Searle, *Speech Acts* (Cambridge: Cambridge University Press, 1969).

Carol Feldman, "Pragmatic Features of Natural Language," in M. W. LaGaly, R. A. Fox, and A. Bruck, eds., *Papers from the Tenth Regional Meeting of the Chicago Linguistic Society* (Chicago: Chicago Linguistic Society, 1974).

Charles Fillmore, "The Case for Case Reopened," in P. Cole and J. Saddock, eds., *Syntax and Semantics. Vol. 8: Grammatical Relations* (New York: Academic Press, 1977).

p. 87 Morris, *Signs, Language, and Behavior.*

Gerald Gazdar, *Pragmatics: Implicature, Presupposition, and Logical Form* (New York: Academic Press, 1979).

p. 89 Henri Zukier and Albert Pepitone, "Social Roles and Strategies in Prediction: Some Determinants of the Use of Base Rate Information," *Journal of Personality and Social Psychology* 47, no. 2 (Aug. 1984). Quotations from p. 349.

Daniel Kahneman, Paul Slovic, and Amos Tversky, ***Judgment under Uncertainty: Heuristics and Biases*** (Cambridge: Cambridge University Press, 1982).

p. 90 Jerome Bruner, Jacqueline Goodnow, and George Austin, ***A Study of Thinking*** (New York: Wiley, 1956).

p. 92 The study of "dramatic concepts" is still in progress and unpublished.

7. Nelson Goodman's Worlds

p. 93 This chapter was prepared for the ***New York Review of Books*** and was in press when this book was printed.

This chapter is based principally on three books by Nelson Goodman: ***Of Mind and Other Matters*** (Cambridge, Mass.: Harvard University Press, 1984); ***Ways of Worldmaking*** (Hassocks, Sussex: Harvester Press, 1978); ***Languages of Art: An Approach to a Theory of Symbols*** (Indianapolis and Cambridge: Hackett, 1976). Quotations, unless otherwise specified, are from ***Of Mind and Other Matters.***

p. 95 For an account of the cognitive revolution see Howard Gardner, ***The Mind's New Science: A History of the Cognitive Revolution*** (New York: Basic Books, 1985).

Rudolph Carnap, ***Der Logische Aufbau der Welt*** (Berlin: Welkreis-Verlag, 1928).

Carl Hempel, ***Fundamentals of Concept Formation in Empirical Science*** (Chicago: University of Chicago Press, 1952); idem, ***Philosophy of Natural Science*** (Englewood Cliffs, N.J.: Prentice-Hall, 1966).

p. 96 Immanuel Kant, ***The Critique of Pure Reason,*** trans. Norman Kemp Smith (New York: St. Martin's Press, 1965).

David Hume, ***A Treatise of Human Nature*** (London and New York: J. M. Dent and Sons Ltd. and E. P. Dutton and Co., 1911).

p. 97 Noam Chomsky, ***Aspects of the Theory of Syntax*** (Cambridge, Mass.: M.I.T. Press, 1965).

Barbel Inhelder and Jean Piaget, ***The Growth of Logical Thinking from Childhood to Adolescence*** (New York: Basic Books, 1958).

Alan Newell and Herbert Simon, ***Human Problem Solving*** (Englewood Cliffs, N.J.: Prentice-Hall, 1972).

Philip N. Johnson-Laird, *Mental Models: Toward a Cognitive Science of Language, Inference, and Consciousness* (Cambridge, Mass.: Harvard University Press, 1983).

p. 98 Clifford Geertz, *Local Knowledge: Further Essays in Interpretive Anthropology* (New York: Basic Books, 1983).

p. 100 W. V. O. Quine, "Other Worldly," *New York Review of Books* (Nov. 23, 1978).

p. 103 E. D. Adrian, *The Basis of Sensation* (London: Christophers, 1928).

Howard Gardner, *Frames of Mind: The Theory of Multiple Intelligences* (New York: Basic Books, 1983).

8. Thought and Emotion

p. 106 Edward Tolman, *Purposive Behavior in Animals and Men* (New York: The Century Company, 1932); see also his "A Reply to Professor Guthrie," *Psychological Review* 45 (1938): 163–164.

George Boole, *An Investigation of The Laws of Thought on Which are Founded the Mathematical Theories of Logic and Probabilities* (New York: Dover Publications, an undated facsimile of the original 1854 ed.).

p. 108 Walter Ong, "The Language and Thought of Print" (a Schweitzer Lecture delivered at New York University, March 1985).

Werner Jaeger, *Early Christianity and Greek Paideia* (Cambridge, Mass.: Harvard University Press, 1961).

Harry Austryn Wolfson, *Religious Philosophy: A Group of Essays* (Cambridge, Mass.: Harvard University Press, 1961).

Etienne Gilson, *Reason and Revelation in the Middle Ages* (New York: Charles Scribner's Sons, 1938).

p. 109 Barbel Inhelder and Jean Piaget, *The Growth of Logical Thinking from Childhood to Adolescence* (New York: Basic Books, 1958).

Robert Woodworth, "Reenforcement of Perception," *American Journal of Psychology,* 1947, 60, 119–124.

p. 110 John Austin, *How to Do Things with Words* (Oxford: Oxford University Press, 1962).

p. 111 Robert Yerkes and J. D. Dodson, "The Relation of Strength of Stimulus to Rapidity of Habit-Formation," *Journal of Comparative and Neurological Psychology* 18 (1908): 459–482.

Karl Muenzinger, "Vicarious Trial and Error at a Point of Choice," *Journal of Genetic Psychology* 53 (1938): 75–86.

p. 112 Jerome Bruner, Jean Matter, and Miriam L. Papanek, "Breadth of Learning as a Function of Drive Level and Mechanization," *Psychological Review* 42 (1955): 1–10; see also R. M. Church, "Effect of Overtraining on Subsequent Learning of Incidental Cues," *Psychological Reports* 2 (1956): 247–254. His paper places constraints on the effect discussed. Also relevant is Jerome Bruner, Jean Matter Mandler, Donald O'Dowd, and Michael Wallach, "The Role of Overlearning and Drive Level in Reversal Learning," *Journal of Comparative and Physiological Psychology* 51 (1958): 607–613.

p. 113 Silvan Tompkin's work is perhaps best illustrated by his *Affect, Imagery and Consciousness,* vol. 1: *The Positive Affects,* and vol. 2: *The Negative Affects* (New York: Springer, 1962, 1963). His more recent views are given in the following two papers: "Affect as Amplification: Some Modifications in Theory," in R. Plutchik and H. Hellerman, eds., *Theories of Emotion* (New York: Academic Press, 1980); and "The Quest for Primary Motives: Biography and Autobiography of an Idea," *Journal of Personality and Social Psychology* 41 (1981): 306–329. For a balanced general account of the study of emotion and its relation to cognitive processes, see George Mandler, *Mind and Body: Psychology of Emotion and Stress* (New York: Norton, 1984).

p. 114 Dan Sperber and Deirdre Wilson, "Mutual Knowledge and Relevance in Theories of Comprehension," in N. V. Smith, ed., *Mutual Knowledge* (London: Academic Press, 1977).

Aidan Macfarlane, *The Psychology of Childbirth* (Cambridge, Mass.: Harvard University Press, 1977).

p. 115 L. A. Sroufe and J. P. Wunsch, "The Development of Laughter in the First Year of Life," *Child Development* 43 (1972): 1326–44.

Daniel Stern, *The Interpersonal World of the Infant* (New York: Basic Books, 1985).

Christopher Pratt, "The Socialization of Crying" (D.Phil. diss., Oxford University, 1978).

p. 116 For a discussion of the James-Lange theory of emotion and alternative views, see Mandler, *Mind and Body.*

Vladimir Bogoraz, *The Chuckchee,* Jessup North Pacific Expedition Publications, no. 7 (New York: American Museum of Natural History, undated rpt. of 1909 ed.).

p. 117 For studies of the induction of emotion produced by the injection of adrenalin and related substances, see Stanley Schachter and Jerome Singer, "Cognitive, Social and Physiological Determinants of Emotional State," *Psychological Review* 69 (1962): 379–399; see also Mandler, *Mind and Body.*

9. The Language of Education

p. 121 A version of this chapter appeared in *Social Research* 49, no. 4 (1982): 835–853.

p. 123 Marcel Granet, *La Pensée chinoise* (Paris: Renaissance du Livre, 1934).

John Fairbank and I conducted an informal seminar at Harvard in 1962 on the "psychology of China," at which he presented a paper on "legitimacy."

p. 125 See particularly Michael Cole and Barbara Means, *Comparative Studies of How People Think: An Introduction* (Cambridge, Mass.: Harvard University Press, 1981); and Michael Cole and Sylvia Scribner, *Culture and Thought: A Psychological Introduction* (New York: Wiley, 1974).

Hugh Mehan, *Learning Lessons: Social Organization in the Classroom* (Cambridge, Mass.: Harvard University Press, 1979).

Michael A. K. Halliday, *Learning How to Mean* (London: Edward Arnold, 1975).

Roman Jakobson, "Linguistics and Poetics," in *Selected Writings,* III (The Hague: Mouton, 1981).

p. 126 Carol Feldman and James Wertsch, "Context Dependent Properties of Teachers' Speech," *Youth and Society* 8 (1976): 227–258.

p. 127 John Searle, *Speech Acts* (Cambridge: Cambridge University Press, 1969).

Jerome Bruner, "The Act of Discovery," *Harvard Educational Review* 31 (1961): 21–32.

Jean Piaget, *To Understand Is to Invent,* trans. George-Anne Roberts (New York: Grossman, 1973).

p. 128 Wolfgang Iser, *The Act of Reading* (Baltimore: Johns Hopkins University Press, 1978).

p. 129 Jerome Bruner, *The Process of Education* (Cambridge, Mass.: Harvard University Press, 1961).

p. 131 Roland Barthes, *Mythologies* (New York: Hill and Wang, 1972), pp. 53–55.

Cole and Scribner, *Culture and Thought.*

p. 132 Mehan, *Learning Lessons.*

Allan Collins, "Teaching Reasoning Skills," in S. F. Chipman, J. W. Segal, and R. Glaser, *Thinking and Learning Skills,* vol. 2 (Hillsdale, N.J.: Erlbaum, 1985).

10. Developmental Theory as Culture

p. 135 Peter Medawar's *mot* appeared in a letter to *The Times* of London in which he deplored the brawling quality of one of the periodic debates on the "nature versus nurture" controversy raging in the correspondence columns of that paper.

Herbert Simon, *The Sciences of the Artificial* (Cambridge, Mass.: M.I.T. Press, 1969).

p. 136 Crane Brinton, *The Anatomy of Revolution* (New York: Vintage Books, 1957). Quotation from p. 47.

J. B. Bury, *The Idea of Progress: An Inquiry into Its Origin and Growth* (New York: Macmillan, 1932).

p. 137 Benjamin Franklin, "The Charter of Germantown Friends School," in Robert Ulich, ed., *Three Thousand Years of Educational Wisdom: Selections from Great Documents,* 2nd ed. (Cambridge, Mass.: Harvard University Press, 1954).

p. 138 Perry Miller, *Errand into the Wilderness* (Cambridge, Mass.: Harvard University Press, 1956).

p. 139 For a particularly perceptive analysis of Freud's language and imagery, see Paul Ricoeur, *Freud and Philosophy: An Essay on Interpretation* (New Haven: Yale University Press, 1970); see also, in the same interpretive spirit, the essays of Ricoeur and others in Paul Rabinow and William Sullivan, eds., *Interpretive Social Science: A Reader* (Berkeley: University of California Press, 1979). Louis Breger, personal communication.

Sigmund Freud, *The Future of an Illusion* (New York: Norton, 1975).

p. 140 Richard Rorty, "Freud and Reason" (Schweitzer Lecture, New York University, Winter 1984).

p. 141 The best selection from Piaget's enormous *oeuvre* is provided in Howard Gruber and Jacques Voneche, eds., *The Essential Piaget* (New

York: Basic Books, 1977). For an excellent overview of his work, see Margaret Boden, *Jean Piaget* (New York: Viking, 1979).

For references to Vygotsky, see the notes to Chapter 5.

Paulo Freire, *Pedagogy of the Oppressed* (New York: Continuum, 1970).

Ivan Illich, *Deschooling Society* (New York: Harper and Row, 1971).

p. 142 Stephen Toulmin, "The Mozart of Psychology," *New York Review of Books,* Sept. 28, 1978.

p. 143 Baudouin de Courtenay was a particular hero for Jakobson; see Jakobson, *Six Lectures on Sound and Meaning,* with a preface by Claude Lévi-Strauss (Cambridge, Mass.: M.I.T. Press, 1978).

p. 144 The biographical and critical literature on Freud is, of course, enormous. The best one can do is to sample the widely variant interpretations of his work that have been offered. A first sampling that catches the variety might include Philip Rieff, *Freud: The Mind of the Moralist,* 3rd ed. (Chicago: University of Chicago Press, 1979); Ernest Jones, *The Life and Work of Sigmund Freud* (New York: Basic Books, 1953); and Frank Sulloway, *Freud, Biologist of the Mind: Beyond the Psychoanalytic Legend* (New York: Basic Books, 1979).

John Austin, *How to Do Things with Words* (Oxford: Oxford University Press, 1962).

Barbel Inhelder and Jean Piaget, *The Growth of Logical Thinking from Childhood to Adolescence* (New York: Basic Books, 1958).

p. 146 Hans Kohut, *The Restoration of the Self* (New York: International Universities Press, 1977).

Three current critiques of Freud's "archaeological" premise are worth special note: Donald Spence, *Narrative Truth and Historical Truth: Meaning and Interpretation in Psychoanalysis* (New York: Norton, 1982); Roy Schafer, *Narrative Actions in Psychoanalysis* (Worcester, Mass.: Clark University Press, 1981); and Merton Gill, "Metapsychology Is Not Psychology," in M. M. Gill and P. S. Holzman, eds., *Psychology vs. Metapsychology.* Psychological Issues Monograph 36, 1976.

Henri Zukier, "Freud and Development: The Developmental Dimension of Psychoanalytic Theory," *Social Research* 52 (1985): 3–41.

p. 147 Ferdinand de Saussure, *Cours de linguistique générale* (Paris: Payot, 1972). For a particularly penetrating discussion of the limits of structuralism in linguistics generally and in literary theory in particular, see Anatoly Liberman, Introduction to Vladimir Propp, *Theory and History of Folklore* (Minneapolis: University of Minnesota Press, 1984).

A. Colby, L. Kohlberg, J. Gibb, and M. Lieberman, "A Longitudinal Study of Moral Judgment," *Monographs of the Society for Research in Child Development* 48, nos. 1–2 (1983).

Howard Gruber, *Darwin on Man: A Psychological Study of Scientific Creativity* (Chicago: University of Chicago Press, 1981).

Afterword

p. 151 Robert Scholes, *Textual Power: Literary Theory and the Teaching of English* (New Haven: Yale University Press, 1985).

p. 152 Matthias Flacius (1520–1575) was a principal hermeneuticist of the early Reformation, and his injunction regarding the historical roots of Scripture was principally addressed to the indiscipline of the Anabaptist revolt. The doctrine was formulated in the *Catalogus testium veritatis* (1556).

p. 153 For a discussion of Rashi's impact on Christian Biblical interpretation, see Herman Hailperin's excellent account in his *Rashi and the Christian Scholars* (Pittsburgh: University of Pittsburgh Press, 1963). Hailperin also discusses Nicholas of Lyra (1270?–1349), who patterned his interpretative doctrine so closely on Rashi (1040?–1105) that he was called by his detractors "the Ape of Rashi." This age of interpretive zeal (roughly 1250–1350) produced a flowering of scholarship on moral as well as intellectual issues. Among the greats of the period were Albertus Magnus, Aquinas, Duns Scotus, William of Occam, Roger Bacon, and Marsilius of Padua—all morally committed theologians, yet deeply rooted in a tradition of interpretation quite as vigorous as the one through which we are living today.

The remarks of Matisse and Picasso are quoted from Todorov's review.

For a succinct account of Luther's division of the universe into the two kingdoms, and of the role of reason and faith in each, see B. A. Gerrish's piece on Martin Luther in the *Encyclopedia of Philosophy*, vol. 5 (New York: Macmillan, 1967).

p. 154 Albert J. Guerard, *Conrad the Novelist* (Cambridge, Mass.: Harvard University Press, 1958).

Roland Barthes, *S/Z: An Essay,* trans. Richard Miller (New York: Hill and Wang, 1974); this volume also includes Balzac's *Sarrasine.*

p. 155 For an account of Odo of Cluny, see Hailperin, *Rashi and the Christian Scholars,* p. 256. Angelom of Luxeuil is also discussed by Hailperin (p. 256) and in more detail by Beryl Smalley, *The Study of the Bible in the Middle Ages* (Notre Dame: University of Notre Dame Press, 1964).

Christopher Ricks, *Milton's Grand Style* (Oxford: Clarendon Press, 1963).

Credits

Grateful acknowledgment is made for permission to quote from the following works:

"Nelson Goodman's Worlds," reprinted with permission from *The New York Review of Books,* copyright © 1986 by Nyrev, Inc.

T. S. Eliot, "The Love Song of J. Alfred Prufrock," in *Collected Poems, 1909–1962* by T. S. Eliot, copyright 1936 by Harcourt Brace Jovanovich, Inc.; copyright © 1963, 1964 by T. S. Eliot; reprinted by permission of Harcourt Brace Jovanovich, Inc., and Faber and Faber Ltd.

James Joyce, "Clay," from *Dubliners* by James Joyce, copyright 1916 by B. W. Huebsch; definitive text copyright © 1967 by the Estate of James Joyce; reprinted by permission of Viking-Penguin, Inc.

Louis MacNeice, "The Sunlight on the Garden," in *Collected Poems, 1925–1948* by Louis MacNeice (London: Faber and Faber, 1949); reprinted by permission of Faber and Faber Ltd.

Czeslaw Milosz, "Ars Poetica?" in *Bells in Winter* by Czeslaw Milosz (New York: Ecco Press, 1978); reprinted by permission of Ecco Press.

William Butler Yeats, "The Sorrow of Love," in *The Poems of W. B. Yeats,* ed. Richard J. Finneran (New York: Macmillan, 1983); reprinted by permission of Macmillan Publishing Co., Inc.

Index